EUARE 2

EUARE LECTURES
SECOND ANNUAL CONFERENCE
2019

Edited by Jocelyne Cesari

EuARe Executive Committee: Karla Boersma, Francesca Cadeddu, Jocelyne Cesari, Silvio Ferrari, Vincente Fortier, Hans-Peter Grosshans, Pantelis Kalaitzidis, Frederik Pedersen, Herman Selderhuis

EUROPEAN ACADEMY OF RELIGION

EUARE LECTURES
Francesca Cadeddu, Series Editor

Graphic Design Project   Cristina Barone
www.europeanacademyofreligion.org

in cooperation with

MINISTERO DELL'ISTRUZIONE DELL'UNIVERSITA' E DELLA RICERCA

Opera realizzata con il supporto di

 Ministero per i beni e le attività culturali e per il turismo   Regione Emilia-Romagna    ASSOCIAZIONE PER LO SVILUPPO DELLE SCIENZE RELIGIOSE IN ITALIA

First Edition 2020
ISBN 978-88-96118-02-3

© 2020 by Fondazione per le scienze religiose Giovanni XXIII
via San Vitale 114
40125 Bologna

All rights reserved. No part of this work may be reproduced or utilized in any form or by any means, electronic or mechanical, including photocopying, recording, or any information storage and retrieval system, without prior written permission from the publisher.

Contents

- 9   Introduction ∼ Jocelyne Cesari
- 19   Secularism and Social Transformation ∼ Craig Calhoun
- 57   Conceptions of Self and Community in Social Ethics: What Place for Religion? ∼ Maureen Junker-Kenny
- 75   Individuals and Communities: What Did Jewish Contemporary Thought Bring to Political Theory? ∼ Sophie Nordmann
- 95   In Search of a Contemporary Sharī'a Discourse of Pluralism ∼ Tim Winter
- 135   Notes on Contributors
- 139   Name Index

EUARE LECTURES

Introduction
Jocelyne Cesari

By assuming multiple interactions between the individual and the community, the overarching goal of the 2019 EuARe Annual Conference – entitled "Empowering the Individual, Nurturing the Community" – was to foster an interdisciplinary exploration of how these interactions shape religious traditions across time and cultural contexts. In some cases, the individual and the community move in opposite directions: the empowered individual privileges his/her interests over the community's common good and, by contrast, the community can impose one dominant mode of being over all individuals. In fact, in our Western democracies, there is a growing concern that individual rights are at risk under the rise of the religious or cultural demands of groups. At the same time, the never-ending demands for the protection of individual rights, from health to economy to culture, are often decried as factors in the weakening of democratic governance and the erosion of the common good. The four keynote lectures presented in this volume shed light on the different and somewhat contradictory positions on the individual and communities from the perspectives of different disciplines and religious traditions, with Maureen Junker-Kenny and Craig Calhoun addressing the tension between individual and community from the point of view of political theory and sociology respectively.

Interestingly, none of these lectures questions the dichotomy between the individual and the religious community. Not surprisingly, the four keynote speakers are persons of their time, meaning that they all expressed the modern ideal of relegating religion outside the regulation of the community. Such an assumption stands in sharp contrast to the pre-modern understanding of community so efficiently captured by Émile Durkheim.[1] Until modernisation, there is no religion outside the community or, to say it differently, the significant distinction is between sacred and profane. The sacred represents the unity of a religious group through collective symbols while, in contrast, the profane refers to mundane personal matters. This distinction was central to pre-modern religious communities which were also political, in the Aristotelian sense of the term. It means that there was no distinction between religious beliefs, institutions, agents and the *polis* or political community. In this perspective, religion was key to the distribution of power, the cohesion and identification of the group to collective symbols. In modern times, the sacred/profane divide has been displaced by the

---

[1] É. Durkheim, *The Elementary Forms of the Religious Life* (New York: The Free Press, 1995).

secular/religious one. This shift signifies that the secular nation defines the collective political unity while religion is perceived primarily as personal beliefs. A brief history of the secular/religious distinction may clarify this assertion. The secular was a category developed within Latin Christendom in the aftermath of the Wars of Religion. *Saeculum* or profane time was contrasted with eternal sacred time.[2] In Latin, *saeculum* meant a fixed period of time, roughly one hundred years or so. In the Romance languages, it evolved into century. After the Wars of Religion, it became used to contrast this temporal age of the world from the divinely eternal realm of God.[3] Anything secular has to do with earthly affairs rather than with spiritual affairs.

As a consequence, certain places, institutions, persons and functions were inscribed within one or the other times. The transfer of certain properties and institutions from church control to the state was therefore secularisation. For the first time since the establishment of the Catholic Church, the political community could exist outside the divine guidance of the pope and be defined on its own terms. From this moment on, secularisation in Western Europe has never ceased, not simply at the institutional level but most importantly at the societal level, leading to today's dominant perception that 'this worldly'

---

[2] E. Mendieta/J. Beaumont, "Reflexive Secularization", in J. Beaumont (ed.), *The Routledge Handbook of Postsecularity* (New York: Routledge, 2018) 425–436.
[3] Ibid.

is all there is, and that the higher 'other worldly' is the product of the human community. This shift led to two major changes: first, the concept of good political order and social virtues was disconnected from Christian ethics; second, the division of labour between the immanent (secular) and the transcendent (religious) was theologically acknowledged. Needless to say, the existence of the immanent and transcendent is constitutive of Christianity, but until the pre-modern era the church was in charge of the two levels or, in Augustine terms, the two cities. After the Wars of Religion, the church delegated its guidance of the immanent to the political power. This division of labour was the invention of Latin Christendom and, incidentally, constituted Christendom's contribution to the process of secularisation.[4] The Western understanding of the secular builds on this separation. It affirms, in effect, that the 'lower' immanent or secular order is all that there is and that the 'higher', or transcendent, order does not exist to regulate the 'lower'. The believers are therefore expected to keep the transcendent to themselves and not let belief influence the political or social practices in which they are engaged. This separation was accelerated through the Reformation, laying the groundwork for the ascendance of a neutral, self-sufficient secular order and leading to the contemporary situation where belief in God is considered to be one among several viable spiritual options.

[4] C. Taylor, *A Secular Age* (Cambridge, MA: Harvard University Press, 2007).

Simultaneously, the nation became the superior collective identification that took precedence over religious allegiances, which from then on could only be individual. Religion became the domain of personal spirituality while all collective allegiances were oriented toward the nation as a sovereign community of individuals equal in rights.

The secular/religious distinction took precedence over the sacred/profane, i.e. the sacred/profane divide has been displaced by the secular/religious one, where the secular nation is the cornerstone of the group unity while religion becomes personal spirituality. At the same time, the sacred has not disappeared in secular nations. It now refers to both political and religious symbols: the flag, national anthem, memorials, places of worship and shrines, rituals and time. The interactions between the secular and the religious are never-ending and determine the modern role of religion *vis-à-vis* community, which is not reflected in our current approach to individual and community, which are by default seen as conflictual, especially when religion is concerned.

Owing to the influence of the European history on political theories, modernisation has been defined as a separation between the 'this worldly' and the 'other worldly', relegating religion to personal faith and beliefs with no direct implication on society and politics, although this relegation does not reflect the reality of religion in advanced secular democracies as attested by numerous empirical surveys. Moreover, the triad modernisation-privatisation-democratisation has served as the golden standard of political development outside the West. For this reason, the classification of religious forms of life in political science casts them almost exclusively as ideological phenomena that are identified and studied primarily as ideas or beliefs. Such an approach reduces religion to rhetoric for political mobilisation and gives the illusion that the knowledge of concepts and symbols in religious traditions is the principal or only way to understand their role in politics. Scholarship in theology and the study of religion that accords pre-eminence to textual analysis has reinforced that tendency and contributed to decontextualised approaches to religion, as if ideas or beliefs alone determine political situations. As a consequence, two other dimensions of religion (belonging and behaving) are neglected in the political analysis, while they are in some cases more significant than the belief itself.

Sophie Nordmann and Tim Winter's lectures highlight how this modern understanding of community and individual has transformed Judaism and Islam. The alignment between the religious message, the people and the (lost) territory of Zion remained engrained in the diasporic Jewish narrative and consciousness, partly due to their segregation from European pre-modern societies. However, the rise of modern nation-states and the political emancipation of Jews created a tension between belonging to the Jewish people and to the territory given by God. The religious reformists of the nineteenth century addressed these tensions by according precedence to personal religiosity over belonging to Zion. In the same vein, Theodor Herzl's conception of the nation reflects this modern split between political community and religious individuals since, in his view, the future Israelis did not have to embrace religious ideas and values to be citizens of the new nation. In this respect, one can read the current politics of Israel as an exemplification of the tensions between the ideal of the religious community (Zion) within the confines of a modern nation.

Within the Islamic tradition, the alignment between religious and political community was embodied in the Medina experience. Under the guidance of the prophet Muhammad, Christians and Jews were included in the Medina community alongside Muslims. After the death of the prophet and the rise of Muslim empires, caliphs acknowledged the religious and cultural diversity of their populations. Those living within the Muslim empires, whether Muslims, Christians, Jews, Zoroastrians, Bahá'ís or Druzes, were included in the *umma* regardless of religious or ethnic background. In this perspective, the abode of Islam or *dār al-Islām*, opposed to *dār al-harb* (the abode of war, i.e. the non-Muslim world) was not innately territorial. Rather, as expressed by Manoucher Parvin and Maurie Sommer, it was "a legal construct that has a territorial dimension: [...] a political-territorial expression of that community in which the Islamic religion is practiced and where it is protected by a Muslim ruler. [...] In the *dār al-harb*, though Islam might be practiced, it does not enjoy the protection of the non-Muslim ruler".[5]

---

[5] M. Parvin/M. Sommer, "Dar al-Islam: The Evolution of Muslim Territoriality and Its Implication for Conflict Resolution in the Middle East", *International Journal of Middle East Studies* 11 (1980) 1–21, on pp. 4–5.

Western influence and the concept of nations shifted the balance among religious traditions within the *umma* and resulted in conflicting intellectual and political movements such as Pan-Islamism, which was influenced by the European concepts of individuals and community. These modern understandings redefined tradition (*taqlīd*) in such a way as to make the past knowledge and concepts irrelevant to the present.[6] Similarly, the historical plural conception of the *umma* was replaced by the community of all Muslims across nations. In other words, *dār al-Islām* and *umma* became synonymous. Following the fall of the Ottoman Empire, the rise of nation-states went hand in hand with religious, linguistic and cultural homogenisation, excluding or even destroying religious, or ethnic, populations which did not belong to the dominant group in power. As a consequence, one form of Islam became the major feature of the new political community.

The transformation of Islam and Judaism in modern times sheds light on the pre-eminence attributed to individual salvation over the revelation-based community. Although such a pre-eminence remains an acute site of contestation, it has nevertheless deeply transformed theological debates and doctrines. In other words, like Christianity in Europe at the time of the Reform, Judaism and Islam have seen not only their political and social influence but also their doctrinal content redefined to make

---

[6] Cf. K.S. Vikør, *Between God and the Sultan: A History of Islamic Law* (Oxford: Oxford University Press, 2006).

room for state sovereignty over mundane matters and limit God's sovereignty to the guidance of souls. The modern divide between religion and politics has also deeply transformed non-monotheistic traditions, as was debated in the conference. It is within this modern dichotomy that religious individuals now have to posit their allegiance to both their religious and their political communities, with all the challenges discussed in detail by our four keynote speakers.

Secularism and Social Transformation
Craig Calhoun

What Max Weber called the differentiation of value spheres has been fundamental not just for modern social thought but for modernity itself. It is a basis for distinction of academic disciplines, for ideologies like the notion of a free market sharply distinct from politics and states, and for the relegation of religion to private life or a space somehow separate from the rest of social life. This effort to differentiate has influenced both social imaginaries and material institutions. But it also distorts efforts to observe modernity.

The idea of secularisation is a case in point. It commonly incorporates a notion of complete neutrality, a view from nowhere and always. However, we have no vantage point outside history from which to look at ostensible secularisation with perfect objectivity and from an undistorted perspective. Do we look from a position of faith, or unbelief, or vague religious identity without consistent practice? Each has been shaped by the history of secularisation. Do we look from the viewpoint of universities? These are deeply implicated in the very changes we would seek to understand. Do we look as citizens of modern states? These are deeply shaped by both ideologies of political secularism and efforts to enforce it through purges of religion from the public sphere (as previously of minority religions). Do we look from the vantage point of international relations? We cannot escape a history of political theology, thinking about sovereignty as the radical autonomy of national states, and of relations among states as limited to instrumental agreements or conflicts.

The idea of secularisation focuses attention on certain questions and obscures others. We ask about the presence or absence of religion in international relations, in state operations, in public life, in science or knowledge, and in the practices of individuals. We ask whether states should recognise religion at all, and if they do, how they can achieve fairness among religions or between the religious and non-religious. We ask about the sources, virtues and limits of tolerance. We ask whether religion needs to be defended, or opposed, or will fade of its own accord.

Yet the transformations in which questions of secularisation are embedded also involve reconstituting categories of thought that are not narrowly about secularisation or religion.

I began with one example, the idea of distinct spheres of value and societal operations. Arguments about the relationship of politics to economics, for example, tend to take for granted that each is a distinct domain (or value sphere). Each is to be understood internally – as distinct from imagining that religion integrates them with common ideas of value, purpose, commonality – or indeed inevitability and possibility. The idea that politics and economics are discrete domains grew up alongside the 'emancipation' of each from religion, but it influences far more than the degree to which each one is religious.

The issue is not just that we cannot be neutral when we look at secularisation. It is that the organisation of thought bundled in with secularisation encourages us to think such neutrality is possible not only with regard to secularisation, but also in regard to technology, economic organisation, the nature of the human, and the social value of community. We are led to imagine that not only thought but also institutions can in this sense be neutral, disembedded not just from religion but from basic questions of value and perspective.

I want to focus, in line with the theme of this conference, on the related questions of what it means to be human and the relationship between individuality and sociality. These questions need to be addressed in ways that recognise both religious and secular influences as entwined with each other and as constitutive for what we see and sometimes for what we do not.

1. Multiple and Limited Secularisations

The idea of a linear historical process of secularisation was almost taken for granted for most of the twentieth century. Some embraced it, arguing against religious influence in this or that domain. Some sought to resist it. Most did not think about it much, but tacitly assumed some version of a secularisation story. In varying combinations, this story emphasised religion's decline. It was consigned to the realm of private rather than public life and to domestic rather than international politics; and it was compartmentalised apart from other increasingly prominent institutions, including science and markets, but also education, health care, and government itself.

Such accounts were influential among academics, with some variation across disciplines, among a broader range of intellectuals, and among both political and institutional leaders. This was true in the United States where religious participation remained widespread, and religious ritual and symbol remained part of public life, albeit diminished. It was even more prominent in Europe, where formal church attendance declined earlier and more rapidly, and, in some countries more than others, religious symbols were more fully banished from public life. This became a central concern of many religious leaders and organisations, but many still saw it as a master trend.

Recently, however, a number of scholars have questioned whether secularisation was in fact a general facet of modernity. Some have suggested that it was more specific, perhaps a European exception to global trends. Others have demonstrated that secularisation was not so complete or so irreversible even in Europe as was long claimed.

Both sides of this debate have seen secularisation largely through what Charles Taylor has called a "subtraction story".[1] They have pointed out reductions in religious

---

[1] C. Taylor, *A Secular Age* (Cambridge, MA: The Belknap Press of Harvard University Press, 2007), 22.

participation or influence, or they have pointed to ways in which religion still mattered or even mattered anew. In this arithmetic perspective, there was simply more or less religion. If religion did not decline overall, it was confined within some realms of life or social policy and excluded from others. Secularisation was seen as a decline or displacement of religion that left the rest of society more or less as it had been.

This view is mistaken on several dimensions. Undoubtedly, processes that we can call secularisation did take place. Their importance has been fundamental, but secularisation has been part of a much wider transformation than simply a decline in religion. In the first place, religion itself has been remade, not just reduced or marginalised. Second, the institutions, cultures and actors that we regard as not religious have been remade, in some cases ostensibly emancipated from religion, or made anew with a minimal reliance on religion but, in any case, made different in ways beyond a simple reduction of religion. Third, as sharp and significant as the religion/not religion boundary may seem, transformation has produced a remarkable range of hybrids and interrelationships. Fourth, the common notion of secularisation bundles together distinct phenomena that do not always coincide.

Scaling up and increased mediation are central to religion as well as to the secular structures that sometimes compete with religion. The transnational reach of religious communications and organisations has increased, for example, from Western missionary activity through migration-based extensions like global Sikhism to the rise of network Christianity.[2] Islam may have spread with physical movements along trading routes from the Middle East through Asia, but Muslims are now linked by a variety of new media. The Yoido Church beams televised messages to satellite congregations around the world. In these and other processes, religion has been restructured not simply displaced or replaced. Its growth cannot be dismissed as somehow a throwback to the pre-modern. It is part of modernisation (if that word still has meaning).

If the transnational reach of religion has grown, so have the transnational reach of markets, gambling, trafficking and pornography, and both states and international organisations are trying to police each of them. The role of religion has been reduced in many settings, though not clearly not in all. Subtraction stories are misleadingly linear.

Subtraction is a poor description of a marginalisation shaped largely by the expansion of secular power, authority and capacity to organise. The rise of modern states, markets and science-based health care all did effectively drive

---

[2] The phrase "network Christianity" has been used by B. Christerson and R.W. Flory to describe the influence of Charismatic preachers outside denominational religious organisations in the US, cf. B. Christerson/R.W. Flory, *The Rise of Network Christianity: How Independent Leaders Are Changing the Religious Landscape* (New York: Oxford University Press, 2017). They emphasise fluidity and experimentation, not just organisationally but in spiritual practice. At the same time, however, there has also been a growth in efforts to maintain doctrinal purity and authority and in publishing houses, online networks and other supports for religious communication that spread orthodoxy as well as heterodoxy.

religion into different and generally smaller spaces of modern social life, although to a different degree in different places. In Europe, states that were previously protagonists in religious struggles increasingly banished religion from public life and the internal workings of government. But states also thereby took on the task of deciding what is and is not religion. The administration of colonies also committed European states to deciding their policy towards religion and religions. This meant both determining the relationship between colonial and indigenous religions and also simply deciding what counted as religion. This project of administratively recognising diverse religions is arguably the key to the production of the very category of religions.[3] In the US, the plurality of ways to be Christian came to the fore, but eventually there were also questions about other immigrant religions and indigenous religions. The state looked more favourably on religion, but this, too, committed it to the work of demarcation and recognition. For example, religious organisations receive a tax exemption, but this requires the Internal Revenue Service to define what is, and what is not, a religious organisation.[4]

---

[3] T. Masuzawa, *The Invention of World Religions: Or, How European Universalism Was Preserved in the Language of Pluralism* (Chicago/London: University of Chicago Press, 2005). As Masuzawa stresses, this process was also embedded in the academic study of religion and in projects of interfaith dialogue like the Parliament of World's Religions launched in 1893 at Chicago Columbian Exhibition.

[4] D. Podus, "Churches, Tax-Exemption, and the Social Organization of Religion", *Comparative Social Research* 13 (1991) 127–178.

In addition, as Alfred Stepan points out, stabilisation of the relationship between religion and modern states was not a one-way process. At least in democracies, it required recognition and toleration in each direction. Religious leaders recognised state authority and states recognised the legitimacy of at least some forms of religious practice and institutions.[5] But in the very toleration demarcation and boundaries were embedded.

The founders of the US banned establishment of religion not to minimise it but so that it could be free from state control. It was to be free as a matter of individual inspiration and reflection and as a matter of institutionalised practice. This resolved problems integrating colonies in which different Christian denominations had been established or favoured. It also helped to create a marketplace of religion, a free individual choice of congregations, denominations, and practices that may have been responsible for much of the greater flourishing of religion in the US compared to most of Europe.[6]

Over time, the US Constitutional prohibition of established religion came to be understood as requiring

---

[5] A. Stepan, "The Multiple Secularisms of Modern Democratic and Non-Democratic Regimes", in C. Calhoun/M. Juergensmeyer/J. VanAntwerpen (ed.), *Rethinking Secularism* (New York: Oxford University Press, 2011) 114–144.

[6] See W.C. Roof, *Spiritual Marketplace: Baby Boomers and the Remaking of American Religion* (Princeton: Princeton University Press, 2001) building on M.E. Marty, *A Nation of Behavers* (Chicago: University of Chicago Press, 1976) and subsequent work.

a separation of church and state. This doctrine is often taken as definitive of a secular state, but there are important others. In particular, there is a doctrine of fairness. In India, for example, the state funds and legally recognises religion, but is deemed secular by maintaining a principled distance and funding different religions proportionately.[7] In short, there are a variety of different secularisms, both in relation to states and on other dimensions.[8]

2. *Publics*

The intellectual and policy habit that compartmentalises religion in a realm of private life can be taken to imply that religion has simply become less and less public. But this is wrong. Public religion has played a range of constitutive roles in modern life.[9] To take just one, religious nationalism has grown more influential, though it has ebbed and flowed, partly because nationalism itself has been solidified as a dominant structure of modern identities. Hindu mobilisation in India is a pre-eminent example today but we could point to Russian Orthodoxy, Polish Catholicism,

---

[7] R. Bhargava, "The Distinctiveness of Indian Secularism", in T.N. Srinivasan (ed.), *The Future of Secularism* (New Delhi: Oxford University Press, 2006) 20–53. See also R. Bhargava, *Secularism and Its Critics* (New York: Oxford University Press, 2005).
[8] See Calhoun/Juergensmeyer/VanAntwerpen (ed.), *Rethinking Secularism*.
[9] See J. Casanova, *Public Religions in the Modern World* (Chicago: University of Chicago Press, 1994).

and other variants. Equally, though, we could note the challenge transnational Islamism delivers to national state projects seen as corrupt or ineffective.

Public religion is not limited to politics but also expressed in largely apolitical public forms of religious devotion. The *Hajj*, Islamic pilgrimage to Mecca, is not without political significance and significance to the Saudi state's claims of eminence among Muslims. But it remains religious, first and foremost, and is not contained by any political project. It has ancient roots, but it has grown enormously to involve more than two million pilgrims annually, aided by modern transport infrastructure and media representations. The Catholic pilgrimage of Lourdes is neither antique nor declining. It dates from the mid-nineteenth century visions of St Bernadette and today involves some 5 million visitors annually. The Camino de Santiago (or *Peregrinatio Compostellana*) was a medieval pilgrimage recurrently revitalised, particularly since the 1990s. Of course, not all who walk the Way of St James do so out of an explicitly religious motivation, although even for the secular there is something inescapably religious about it (something not eclipsed by use of the word 'spiritual' instead of 'religious').

At the same time, these pilgrimages also support substantial businesses from inns along the way to travel agencies and airlines to help pilgrims reach their starting points. As with medieval cathedrals, religious projects can both be businesses and be the occasion for much more or less secular business activity. It is not only new forms of self-discipline and interior convictions about salvation that can connect religion and economic life, even capitalism.

At the same, religious engagements helped promote the spread of literacy, print media, and debate in the public sphere. It is an oddity of Habermas's famous book *The Structural Transformation of the Public Sphere* that it never discusses religion and that its account starts with the development of literary, market and political publics in the eighteenth century. This reflects the tacit exclusion of religion common in thinking about secular institutions. In fact, there would be a strong case for starting the story of modern publics in the seventeenth century, tracing the story of vernacular literacy to translation and printing of the Bible, seeing the circulation of sermons and tracts as basic to the rise of a larger scale public sphere. Of course, this scaling up and modernisation of the public sphere does not provide a definitive beginning to the story of publics. This would necessarily stretch back to the ancient world and reflect developments in republican thought and practice in the centuries just before and overlapping the Protestant Reformation.[10]

Extending the modern story back at least to the seventeenth century could also remind us of the rise of science itself as a public phenomenon, shaped by invisible colleges

---

[10] This would still be only the Western story, neglecting the forms of publicness developed in China and shaped by Confucian thought, or in the later Arabic caliphates, Persia, and Mughal India, all shaped at once by Islam and by scholarship with its own lineages back to ancient Greece.

of correspondents, new institutions such as Britain's Royal Society, and the insistence that all scientific findings be made public for dispute, testing and correction of errors.[11] Needless to say, there were also other dimensions, even a spatial, architectural one in which a core feature was the development of Europe's towns around public squares like Bologna's Piazza Maggiore. Crucially, there was the rise of the state.

The development of publics (gatherings, networks of communication, spaces and spheres and policies but for the moment let me just say 'publics') was an important feature of European, Western modernity (and many alternative modernities around the world). Religion, and indeed religious conflict, played a central role in this. It is important that religion was part of the story of the formation of the modern public, even the modern secular public, but it is also important that religion was not the whole story.

The constitution of secular public spaces cannot be understood merely in terms of the management of relations to religion, banishing religious argument, insisting on 'translation' of religious discourse into secular terms or providing for neutrality among religions. It is necessary also to ask whether public discourse is to be confined in what Taylor called "the immanent frame", understanding based on science and similar approaches that take the material world as all there is.

---

[11] D. Zaret, "Religion, Science, and Printing in the Public Spheres in Seventeenth-Century England", in C. Calhoun (ed.), *Habermas and the Public Sphere* (Cambridge, MA: MIT Press, 1992) 212–235.

Religions can appear simply in the form of identities claimed by actors demanding voice or power in public matters. It can then be managed as a potential power.

Needless to say, however, to speak of religion is not only to speak of a contender for power. Religion is also an effort to understand and to seek deeper meaning. If we cannot find room for religion in public discourse, can we benefit from religious traditions as a source for rethinking the human, for rethinking value, for rethinking the social order? Moreover, will efforts to manage religion stifle other forms of moral imagination and indeed imagination of what is possible, with or without divine inspiration?

As I have argued, the disciplining of publicness to exclude or manage religion was never simply a subtraction of religion. It was a transformation. We need to ask what else was disciplined to the margins along with religion. It was not only divine inspiration that was made suspect in the particular formation of modern publics as, ideally, spheres of rational-critical debate on subjects of material policy concern for modern states. It was also human imagination.

3. *Scale*

At the same time that religious practices, communities and authorities were transformed to produce a secular age, and publics became a central feature of that age, the scale of societal organisation grew enormously. Certainly, there were far-flung empires and long-distance trade before the modern era. But our era has been constituted partly by the building of infrastructures and systems that enable social organisation on an unprecedented and very large scale. We produce the food to feed 8 billion human beings, most of whom now live in cities. At least 20 of those cities have more than 15 million inhabitants (though there are debates on exactly how to count them). There are nodes in transportation and communications systems that connect all the continents of the world and connect the actions of each person to others in a constant work of coordination and sometimes conflict.

These systems are in some degree self-moving or automatic as the movements of prices in relation to supply and demand can proceed without the intervention of king or politicians in Adam Smith's famous image of the invisible hand. This is a difference in kind that is closely related to difference in scale. It is not just that there are more people, in more widely dispersed social relations. The development of socio-technical systems that are at least partially auto-poetic transforms human relatedness. We have relationships with other people whom we confront face-to-face. Some of these are really meaningful relationships such as those which constitute families and communities, some are more casual, like relations with shop clerks. But a growing proportion, indeed by far the majority, are indirect relationships, not only not face-to-face but connecting us to people we do not know and cannot even in principle know. It is not enough to say that modern life is shaped deeply by sociability with strangers, though this is very true, whether we speak of the crowds in a public square at carnival, at an election rally or even of the many anonymous addressees of political speeches. Modern life is also made possible, and deeply shaped, by relationships organised through socio-technical systems in which people play roles, but are not sociable, not addressed as persons, even anonymous ones.

Yet there is also power on a new scale. States are bigger and they play different roles. State power is not just coercive power, the kind of power exercised by monarchs who could say "off with her head" like the Queen of Hearts in *Alice's Adventures in Wonderland*, or governments that put people in prison or detention camps as states do in unprecedented numbers today. Militaries and police are important but modern states also wield 'infrastructural power'. They build highways and telecommunication systems, they run schools and hospitals, they provide unemployment insurance and old-age pensions, they subsidise efforts at industrial innovation and international trade, and of course they collect taxes in ways that are not only large-scale but never simply neutral. States exercise their power both in relation to actual persons and in relationship to socio-technical systems.

So do corporations. I have in mind mainly business corporations, but in fact philanthropies and many non-profit organisations also operate as corporations. They also wield power. Some business corporations are in fact larger and more powerful than most states. Apple, Amazon, Google and Facebook (and Huawei, Alibaba, and Tencent) are among the current giants. These are not democratic.

In general, they are not objects of public address in the same way states are (though this is not impossible). When we speak of a public corporation, we mean only one whose shares are traded publicly rather than held exclusively within a private group such as a family.

Scaling up and increased mediation are, if I may be forgiven the word play, powerful secular trends. They have at once been more or less linear over time, echoing the root of the term secular in measurement of worldly time by contrast to eternity. And they have reflected the emergence of socio-technical systems knitting the world together with less and less reference to religion. The issue is not simply whether devotion has declined. It is whether the literal mediation of priests is as important in a world of mass literacy, telephones, TV and new media. To take a simple and obvious example, modern states maintain secular diplomatic corps.

4. Community and Its Limits

All these changes reconstitute the world. In this reconstitution, growth in the number of human beings and in the scale of their settlements and systems of power have been secular trends. They have marched forward in time, never reversed, at least so far, by cycles of retreat to counteract advance. They have shaped our secular experience, that is our experience of the material, temporal world, which if religious we may still contrast to a more eternal or timeless reality. Human beings live longer lives. We live amid constant transformations of technology, of culture, of relationships. We live amid constant, mediated awareness of at least some of what is happening at great distance in the world, but at the same time and we live with an apparent acceleration, a quickening of change. The sociologist Hartmut Rosa has argued that acceleration is the defining feature of the modern era, not just change but its quickening pace. Already 150 years ago, Karl Marx and Friedrich Engels wrote of capitalism that:

> Constant revolutionising of production, uninterrupted disturbance of all social conditions, everlasting uncertainty and agitation distinguish the bourgeois epoch from all earlier ones. All fixed, fast-frozen relations, with their train of ancient and venerable prejudices and opinions, are swept away, all new-formed ones become antiquated before they can ossify. All that is solid melts into air, all that is holy is profane.[12]

One does not have to be a Marxist to see the truth in this characterisation. It still makes sense in our era of smart phones, artificial intelligence and gene editing, of globalisation, instantaneous market updates, and cyberattacks. But we may doubt the conclusion Marx and Engels drew from this, that as a result humanity would be "at last compelled to face with sober senses his real conditions of

---

[12] Karl Marx/Friedrich Engels, *The Communist Manifesto*, ed. J.C. Isaac (New Haven: Yale University Press, 2012), 77.

life, and his relations with his kind".[13] It is far from clear that accelerating growth in scale and constant disruptive change have freed humanity from illusions or compelled us to realism. We seem, for example, to have a very hard time facing "with sober senses" the possible eradication of our "real conditions of life" by climate change and environmental degradation. In fact, this seems to be yet another accelerating process of change and growing scale that we experience as continuing without end.

I do not intend this lecture to be a catalogue of material changes and challenges faced by humanity. Rather, I have tried simply to evoke these and to indicate how integrally connected are the secular trends of worldly transformation and the process we call secularisation. The transformation of the place of religion in the world did not take place independently of all these other transformations.

This broader sense of transformation is necessary, I want to suggest, to fully make sense of the challenges posed today by new appearances of religion in secular public space, and by the terms chosen for the theme of this conference, the individual and the community.

Let me turn to community first. It is misleading to use term community for all the forms of social existence and commitment in our lives, for all that stands as the social counterpoint to individual. But this is what we tend to do when we counter-pose individual to community as the two seemingly self-evidence forms of human existence.

---

[13] Ibid.

Community has its full meaning in webs of relationships that knit human beings to each other in mutual commitments. Community commonly incorporates families, but this need not be part of the definition. We can, for example, meaningfully speak of monastic communities or other communities of faith in which individuals are more autonomously members. We think of community often in its place-based form: the village or small town, paradigmatically, but also the urban neighbourhood or the communities forged within cities by those who share ethnicity or faith or indeed lifestyle choices and choose to make this the basis for interdependence. Place-based communities are particularly important, however, because they anchor a human relationship to nature, and potentially a relationship of care for the endangered natural world.

Contrasting local community to larger scale society was a stable of nineteenth-century social thought, invoking binary oppositions such as *Gemeinschaft* to *Gesellschaft*. These focused attention on transformations not only in the scale but also in the kind of social relationships. Cities, they suggested, were sites of more voluntary association, less sense of community of fate. People were knit together by contracts not statuses. The anonymity of cities allowed new kinds of freedom as people could express different sides of themselves in different contexts. And all of those allowed new levels of individuation.

At the same time, the notion of community was also claimed for trans-local solidarities, pre-eminently those of nations. It is in national publics that questions of religion and secularism are most acute, not at the local level. Here the rhetoric of community necessarily meant something different from the local context. It could not be a matter of densely interconnected relationships. Even small nations of just a few millions far exceeded that possibility. Rather, nations involved categories of people joined by common culture, or legal citizenship, or political sovereignty or subjection. They were built not out of face-to-face relationships but out of mediated relationships and representations.[14] Nation was in this sense a competitor to local community. And political publics came to be organised overwhelmingly in national terms. Sometimes religion has been central to national political identity, and this secular engagement has itself transformed religion. Contemporary Hindu nationalism is an example. But even where we would not speak of specifically religious nationalism, as Benedict Anderson shrewdly observed, the phenomenon of nation (or nationalism) has more in common with public religions than with political ideologies as conventionally understood.[15] It is a creation of culture and emotion, a way of seeing the world and understanding the self, and indeed sacred.

---

[14] The distinction of categorical from relational structures of identity and affiliation has roots in anthropological accounts of clan vs lineage. See S.F. Nadel, *The Theory of Social Structure* (London: Cohen & West, 1957). It was developed by H.C. White; see *Identity and Control: A Structural Theory of Social Action* (Princeton: Princeton University Press, 1992) and applied to the distinction between community and nationalism in C. Calhoun, *Nationalism* (Milton Keynes: Open University Press, 1997).

[15] B. Anderson, *Imagined Communities: Reflections on the Origin and Spread of Nationalism* (London: Verso, 1991).

5. Individuals

Religions – or specific religious actors and movements – were agents in this transformation, not simply its victims. Early in modernity, the forms of personal and public piety previously restricted to religious specialists like monks were extended to lay people. There were increasing calls for active choices and demonstrations of conviction rather than only tacit compliance. Denominational and doctrinal struggles reinforced this trend. The very intensification of religion paradoxically helped lay the conditions for clearer personal or institutional choices not to be religious.

Modern individualism was pioneered partly in this religious transformation. Prayer, professions of belief, and reading of scripture all became increasingly individual. There was increased emphasis on an interior to the self.[16] Max Weber saw shifting understandings of salvation to a new ideology of self-discipline which he thought essential to capitalism.[17] Michel Foucault traced growing

---

[16] C. Taylor, *Sources of the Self: The Making of the Modern Identity* (Cambridge, MA: Harvard University Press, 1989).

[17] M. Weber, *The Protestant Ethic and the Spirit of Capitalism* (New York: Scribner's, 1958 [German original 1905]). Whether Weber got the story exactly right can, of course, be disputed and has been for more than a hundred years. See, e.g., G. Marshall, *In Search of the Spirit of Capitalism: An Essay on Max Weber's Protestant Ethic Thesis* (London: Hutchinson, 1982). *The Protestant Ethic* was one of Weber's early works. He continued to pursue the question of links between religious ethics and economic activity both in the West and in studies of Asian religions, not least as part of his broader inquiry into rationalisation – in which the economic practices of monasteries also figured.

individualism to the interplay of power and knowledge and the internalisation of domination as self-discipline in the transition from religious domination to supposedly humane post-Enlightenment Europe.[18]

But what it is to be a human individual has itself changed, partly because of these changes in societal organisation. We can see something of the shift in the ways nations are imagined and rhetorically constituted. Modern nations may use a vocabulary of family and lineage but they much more basically connect individuals into the whole. It is as though nationality is inscribed into the very body, or at least the personal identity of individuals. In this sense individuals are understood not through their webs of personal relationships, or of roles like parent and child, sister and brother, but as equivalents in a series. Nation is a pre-eminent example of this serial notion of individuals as units in a larger categorical identity, but not the only one. This is also the main way in which individuals are understood as bearers of human rights, as citizens, and as owners of property.

---

[18] Actually, this is Michel Foucault's initial account, prominent for example in *Discipline and Punish: The Birth of the Prison* (New York: Pantheon, 1977). He complemented this with a later account of more positive potentials in rising self-knowledge and self-mastery. See his *History of Sexuality*, especially *The Care of the Self* (vol. 3 of *The History of Sexuality*, New York: Vintage Books, 1988) and the whole series of his late lectures at the Collège de France. On implications for the study of religion, see I. Strenski, "Religion, Power, and Final Foucault", *Journal of the American Academy of Religion* 66, 2 (1988) 345–367.

Each fits with the punctual self of Western modernity, one token of a type, one unit of a whole. But it is in tension with the idea that each of us is possessed of a unique individuality. In different ways, a variety of Western thinkers have distinguished treating other people merely as objects from treating them as subjects of value. Immanuel Kant's argument against taking any other person to be merely means to our ends, our goals and uses, is a prime example. Martin Buber wrestled with the same issue in distinguishing the I/it relationship from the I/Thou. The I/Thou relation involves recognition of the other as a person, as having a spiritual dimension, and thus as a potential path into relationship with God. Emmanuel Levinas develops similar ideas in his notion of alterity.

6. *To Be Human*

Individualistic as modernity is, it has produced social relations on an unprecedented scale and in ways that challenge individuals and direct relations among individuals. Here we come to my last major theme.

What joins human beings in the larger category humanity and what makes humanity of special value? There are a variety of answers in different historical traditions. Religion is central to many of them. But the process of secularisation, and the wider societal transformations to which it is linked, has encouraged the forgetting or hollowing out of some of these. And there are now new challenges.

For example, the book of Genesis tells us that human beings are created in the image of God. This gives rise to long interpretative traditions which I cannot begin to summarise. They take up many ways in which being created in the image of God distinguishes human beings including not least free will, knowledge of good and evil, reason, and the capacity to consciously create, that is, to continue the process of world-making begun but not ended by God's creation.

Then again, also with roots in Genesis, there is the notion of a Great Chain of Being, or of a natural hierarchy intrinsic to creation, in which humans are placed below God and the angels but given dominion "over the fish in the sea and the birds in the sky and over every living creature that moves on the ground" (Gen 1:28). Versions of the Great Chain of Being elaborated the distinct places of different sorts of human beings, lords and serfs for example, in a relational but very hierarchical understanding. They distinguished the human from other living creatures both on earth and in heaven. We are not mere animals, but neither are we gods or angels. We are also living, of course, and thus distinct from the no longer living though they too have a special status in the order of the universe (varying among religious traditions from the veneration of ancestors to souls awaiting elevation from purgatory into heaven).

In many religious traditions a core understanding of being human and human individuality centres on the soul. For Christianity, this stretches back through Augustine to Plato. It shapes thinking about the place of human beings in the natural hierarchy (above other animals and below angels).[19] It informs understandings of Christ as both God and person, of the Eucharist, of the migration of souls, and ultimately in medieval political theology, of the king's two bodies, which in turn becomes a basis for the idea of a corporation as a person.[20] Being an individual and being human are linked through the notion of soul (though there is more to the construction of individual standing as personhood, in law and eventually in citizenship). I do not propose any exposition of this, or of the meaning of eternal soul in relationship to this mortal coil that we might slough off at death, and still less of differences even within the Christian tradition let alone between it and others. But arguably modern Western individualism develops on the basis of notions of the individual identity of souls. There are interesting questions I cannot answer about this changes with new vocabulary sacralising human life as such, rather than souls, or with claims of spirituality rather than specific and soul-cantered religion.

This rhetorical framework for thinking about the human was at once both readily available and influential. It is, for example, the framework in which the sixteenth-century disputations of Valladolid (at least the side represented by Bartolomeo de las Casas) tackled the question

---

[19] A.O. Lovejoy, *The Great Chain of Being: A Study of the History of an Idea* (Cambridge, MA: Harvard University Press, 1976).

[20] E. Kantorowicz, *The King's Two Bodies: A Study in Mediaeval Political Theology* (Princeton: Princeton University Press, 1957).

of whether, or in which sense, the native inhabitants of Spain's New World colonies were human. Did they have eternal souls and thus require care and protection, albeit in a paternalistic understanding, and ultimately efforts at conversion and salvation? Or were they a lesser kind of being, perhaps above animals but less than human, and suited only for labour (as Juan Ginés de Sepúlveda argued)?[21]

Reliance on both the idea of souls and the image of the Great Chain of Being has faded. A notion of natural individuality came to the fore. This was sometimes linked to expressive notions of self, as in the Romantic tradition. This helped inform depth psychologies like psychoanalysis. In the liberal tradition, individuals were fundamentally owners of property and consumers with irreducible tastes; thinking about citizenship was shaped by both ideas.

But by the late twentieth century, the idea of a distinct genetic makeup replaced the idea of soul as the basis for recognising both individuality and humanness. This genetic makeup was regarded as 'natural' and unalterable. If this view is still intuitive to many, it is also under challenge.

---

[21] Sepúlveda's argument was based at least as much on what he took to be offences against nature committed by the indigenous peoples, like human sacrifices. L. Hanke, *All Mankind Is One: A Study of the Disputation between Bartolomé de Las Casas and Juan Ginés de Sepulveda in 1550 on the Intellectual and Religious Capacity of the American Indians* (DeKalb: Northern Illinois University Press, 1974); L.K. Pharo, "The Council of Valladolid: A European Discussion about the Human Dignity of the Peoples of the Americas", in M. Düwell *et al.* (ed.), *The Cambridge Handbook of Human Dignity* (Cambridge: Cambridge University Press, 2014) 95-100.

Techniques of genetic engineering have made rapid strides in recent years. Using CRISPR-Cas9, however, scientists already have the capacity to change the genetic makeup of unborn babies.[22] Parents who are the carrier of genes for potential diseases may be eager to have children born freed from that risk by changes to their genomes. Indeed, vulnerability is an essential part of the human condition, although looking to the circumstances and existential predicaments of humans is different from finding an interior essence. In any case, there is motivation for experimentation on humans. This is illegal in most countries, although regulation may or may not be effective. Famously, though, it has already been done in China where genetically altered babies have been born. Moreover, as Benjamin Hurlbut has suggested, however much the first experimenters have been stigmatised as deviant, pursuing this goal is much more deeply supported in the relevant scientific fields (which are also commercial fields).[23]

---

[22] One of the most important scientists in the field, Jennifer Doudna, describes this as nothing less than achieving the ability to control evolution. J.A. Doudna/S.H. Steinberg, *A Crack in Creation: Gene Editing and the Unthinkable Power to Control Evolution* (Boston: Houghton Mifflin Harcourt, 2017). Of course, as Darwin already noted in *The Origin of Species*, animal breeders long engaged in shaping evolution. His contribution was to show that it could proceed without conscious intervention, either theirs or God's.

[23] J.B. Hurlbut, "Human Genome Editing: Ask Whether, not How", *Nature*, 2 January 2019, available at https://www.nature.com/articles/d41586-018-07881-1 (accessed 25 May 2020). See also J.B. Hurlbut, *Experiments in Democracy: Human Embryo Research and the Politics of Bioethics*

Of course, gene-editing has its own risks. But although there are powerful commercial and governmental interests at issue, scientists largely claim the right and capacity to regulate themselves. This claim to autonomy is directly related to the differentiation of value spheres and the notion that science must be kept free from religion and politics (although the idea of keeping it separate from commerce seems to have lost purchase).

Yes, gene-editing challenges our received notion of the human, and of what is and is not beyond our control. The capacity to alter the genetic code shaping the lives of human individuals raises questions about what it means to think of those individuals as creatures of God or nature. It raises questions about the idea that humans are basically equal or deserving of equal rights. It raises questions about who should have the authority to change the genes of another person. Parents? If so, on what basis? Do they own their offspring? In most regards we think not and generally think the idea of people owning each other repugnant. Should access to the technology be governed by states? Or markets (as is happening in the West)? But can any single state adequately regulate what in a world can be made available to the rich through medical tourism?

(New York: Columbia University Press, 2017) and S. Jasanoff, *Can Science Make Sense of Life?* (Cambridge/Madford, MA: Polity, 2019).

7. Organism and Mechanism

In the seventeenth century, another kind of contrast became increasingly common in efforts to understand what it was to be human: the contrast of man to machine. This was shaped by the search for perpetual motion, the development of mechanical clocks and a craze for developing mechanical birds and all matter of automata. For some, human beings were just a special kind of self-moving machine. For others, the distinction of human self-movement by free will was fundamental. But note something familiar in the issue which appears today in debates about artificial intelligence, though these are commonly impoverished by the thinness of understanding the human. That is, having all but forgotten the notion of soul, having lost faith in both the Great Chain of Being and the idea of creation in the image of God, we are easily drawn into thinking that we are just algorithms, complex structures of code given organic, genetic form on a carbon base rather than rendered on chips in silicon. And so many in the transhumanist movement find it easy to imagine eternal life, not with God, but by virtue of some possible uploading of the contents of their brains into computers.[24] More than a few are investing large sums of money in being frozen to await this rapture.

---

[24] See H. Tirosh-Samuelson, "Transhumanism as a Secular Faith", *Zygon* 47 (2012) 710–734.

In my view, this sort of thinking goes deeply astray in trying to understand what it is to be human, as well as in imagining migration into machines. For many, this is a view of human beings becoming Gods, creators of life.[25] Arguably this is an extension of the biblical notion of being created in the image of God, but it is a quite radical one which presumes the absence of that original God of the Creation described in Genesis. But let me leave the possible theological failings of this view aside and note two other ways in which I think it goes wrong that bear on the notions of individual and community.

First, the idea that as persons we can be reduced to intelligence, or to the processes of our brains, is extremely dubious. Modern neuroscience stresses that our brains are not autonomous and self-contained, that they are part of complex neural systems in which all the parts matter, that our cognition and emotion are influenced also by chemical processes, and that cognitive-neural system works only in relation to our bodies, managing relations to internal and external disturbances, perhaps seeking homeostasis, but in any case, deeply embedded.[26]

Second, the notion that human intelligence is contained within individual brains or even individual bodies is misleading. Human intelligence is the product of sharing and learning, of language and culture, of communication

---

[25] Y.N. Harari, *Homo Deus: A Brief History of Tomorrow* (New York: Harper, 2017).

[26] A. Damasio, *The Strange Order of Things: Life, Feeling, and the Making of Cultures* (New York: Vintage Books, 2018).

and social relationships. The point is not just that our thinking stands on the shoulders of giants (and others) who have gone before. It is that we think in language and in dialogue, not in isolation.

Artificial intelligence may, and probably will, grow dramatically more powerful. It will transform material production and change or eliminate many jobs. It will change the way all the socio-technical systems that connect us work, from transport to water supply to record keeping. It is already changing the work of doctors, lawyers, architects, and policemen. So, I do not mean to suggest it is not powerful. Rather, I want to suggest that processes of automation are largely social process. We began the process of automation not simply with mechanical birds or the first computers but with the modern state, the business corporation, the factor and all the sociotechnical systems that work by establishing workflows, sets of instructions to govern the work of the whole. As Thomas Hobbes wrote on the first page of *Leviathan* what is the state but an artificial person?

> NATURE (the art whereby God hath made and governs the world) is by the art of man, as in many other things, so in this also imitated, that it can make an artificial animal. For seeing life is but a motion of limbs, the beginning whereof is in some principal part within, why may we not say that all automata (engines that move themselves by springs and wheels as doth a watch) have an artificial life? For what is the heart, but a spring; and the nerves, but so many strings; and the joints, but so many wheels, giving

motion to the whole body, such as was intended by the Artificer? Art goes yet further, imitating that rational and most excellent work of Nature, man. For by art is created that great LEVIATHAN called a COMMONWEALTH, or STATE (in Latin, CIVITAS), which is but an artificial man, though of greater stature and strength than the natural, for whose protection and defence it was intended; and in which the sovereignty is an artificial soul, as giving life and motion to the whole body; the magistrates and other officers of judicature and execution, artificial joints; reward and punishment (by which fastened to the seat of the sovereignty, every joint and member is moved to perform his duty) are the nerves, that do the same in the body natural; the wealth and riches of all the particular members are the strength; salus populi (the people's safety) its business; counsellors, by whom all things needful for it to know are suggested unto it, are the memory; equity and laws, an artificial reason and will; concord, health; sedition, sickness; and civil war, death. Lastly, the pacts and covenants, by which the parts of this body politic were at first made, set together, and united, resemble that fiat, or the Let us make man, pronounced by God in the Creation.[27]

Even before the latest advances in machine learning and artificial intelligence, we have long been engaged in creating organisational systems that in some combination

[27] T. Hobbes, *Leviathan* (Harmondsworth: Penguin, 1981), 7.

supplement and supplant human action. In the contemporary world, we place great emotional emphasis on direct interpersonal relationships. But to a very large extent our world is given its structure not by these but rather by indirect relations mediated through technological and organisational systems.[28] We relate to other people not as visible, knowable individuals but obscured in the indirect relationships of complex socio-technical systems some of which seem to move of themselves. Or we relate to them as the serial units of categories (that is to say members of nations) and again not directly as persons. This does not make a stronger recognition of humanness or spiritual communion impossible. We can, for example, approach human rights with ideas of reverence for all human beings, each equally exemplifying the category. But it is a challenge to see the spiritually, sacredly human in, for example, market actors.

It is worth noting, if only in passing, another example of the troubled character of the individual person in the modern world. This is the idea that a corporation is itself an individual. The idea is encouraged in much corporate law (though there are differences in national legal

---

[28] C. Calhoun, "Indirect Social Relations and Imagined Communities", in P. Bourdieu/J.S. Coleman (ed.), *Social Theory for a Changing Society* (Boulder/New York: Westview Press/Russell Sage Foundation, 1991) 95-120 and C. Calhoun, "The Infrastructure of Modernity: Indirect Social Relationships, Information Technology, and Social Integration", in H. Haferkamp/N.J. Smelser (ed.), *Social Change and Modernity* (Berkeley: University of California Press, 1992) 205-236.

traditions). There are competing accounts. Corporations may be understood as merely creatures of contract. They may be seen as concessions or assignments of the authority of the crown or the state. But corporations are distinguished from their investors, managers, and other members. This is integral to notions of limited liability that make modern forms of joint stock ownership possible and with it the trading of shares of ownership in stock markets.

Influential roots of this notion of the business corporation are in fact religious. In canon law, the bishop as owner of church property is a legal (and ecclesiastical) construct separate from the human personhood of the individual incumbent (a 'corporation sole'). The concept is analogous to that of the king's two bodies which enables us to say "the king is dead, long live the king" and ensure the smooth succession of rule as well as property. In secular law, this most directly influences the treatment of private corporations. But this way of thinking about corporations as kinds of persons also creates a fundamental asymmetry between human individuals and these artificial individuals. Like ordinary human beings, at least those of legal age and competency, corporations can own and sell property, enter into contracts, and sue or be sued in courts of law.

By an extraordinary, but perhaps predictable, extension, corporations in the United States are treated as citizens possessed of civil rights. In the decision called *Citizens United v. FEC*, the US Supreme Court famously determined that corporations are entitled to the protection of free speech which the US Constitution granted to citizens, and thus that there should be no limits on their financial contributions to political campaigns. À propos of religion and secularity in matters of public policy, this then becomes one of the arguments deployed to assert that there should be no restrictions on the political activities of religious bodies (though this leaves unaddressed the special status of tax exemption).

8. Conclusion

The rise of the state, the corporation, and the global market all raise anxieties about loss of community and questions about what it means to be a human individual. So do artificial intelligence and genetic engineering. But can these questions be answered entirely within the immanent frame?

The term post-secular grants that there was some time or at least some intellectual consensus when secularity could be presumed, but then suggests that this presumption no longer holds. So secular a thinker as Jurgen Habermas has argued that we must not only accept that religion is part of public life, but ask whether it has potentially valuable, even crucial contributions to make. Religions may contribute specific ideas to contemporary debates, even secular ones.

At the same time, though, the way in which we seek to differentiate the religious and the secular can hamper us in our ability to grasp both the history and the future directions of our society and the choices open to us. How we understand both individual and community, and the rest of human life and society, is deeply shaped by the ways we have produced distinctions between the religious and the secular, as well as simply by religion.

Our self-understandings, our ideas about what it means to be a human being and a person, and our relationships to each other are all potentially of fundamental spiritual importance. For many kinds of relationships, however, this is obscured in our contemporary world. It is by how we think, and by the asymmetry between our directly interpersonal relationships and the organisations and systems that facilitate social organisation at very large scale.

If we lose our capacity to say what it means to be human and why we value humanity, we become inarticulate in a host of other discourses from human rights and citizenship to the ethics and legal regulation of human-altering technologies. Our hopes for both individuality and community are undermined.

Yet, perhaps the most important distinction of being human is the capacity for transcendence. Is it our ability not just to compete economically or to distribute power politically or to invent technologically but to remake ourselves that is most distinctive?

The importance of religious and other imaginations is in part, the effort to transcend the conditions immediately given to us and given to life.[29] This pursuit of transcendence

---

[29] C. Calhoun, "Time, World, and Secularism", in P.S. Gorski *et al.* (ed.), *The Post-Secular in Question: Religion in Contemporary Society* (New York/London: New York University Press) 335–364.

may be secular, a pursuit of a better temporal world. It may be focused on more otherworldly goods. But part of being human is in fact the potential for transcendence, the effort to want to have better desires than those we immediately feel, the effort to make the world and ourselves better than we are.

Conceptions of Self and Community in Social Ethics: What Place for Religion?

Maureen Junker-Kenny

The conference title, "Empowering the Individual, Nurturing the Community", envisions the goal of an optimal correspondence between self and community. The themes explored in its parallel sessions identify the problems to be faced and some of the analyses and means needed to overcome them. The dynamics of each can go in opposite directions: the "empowered individual" can become the choosing rational agent with no concern for others apart from tolerating their ways of living. And "communities" can develop into nurturing but self-centred groupings with interpretations of their identities that are dismissive of others, as examined in this conference's sessions treating populist movements in Europe. Therefore, it cannot be an automatic assumption that religion "empowers the individual" and "nurtures" the senses of community and of justice in a positive way. Religions have shown themselves to be as affected by xenophobia and in-group orientations as other cultural traditions. The hope thus is to encourage and connect justice- and peace-oriented interpretations and movements. How does the public sphere have to be conceptualised and structured in order not to stymie, but instead to enable recognition and cooperation with others on shared problems? These include the effects of technological progress on contemporary and future lifeworlds and the ecological boundaries of the planet, which also force migration from areas that are becoming uninhabitable. The existing unresolved and the emerging issues also require new efforts among the religions in order to work out a level of cohesion that is needed for democratic decision-making. A "culture of listening"[1] oriented towards what the Christian social ethicist David Hollenbach calls "dialogical universalism"[2] needs to be fostered, going beyond the framework of a minimal ethics which only secures negative rights.

I wish to explicate the traditions of thinking involved in the key terms of the conference title by proceeding in four steps. The first three relate to three approaches to social philosophy and ethics: community, contract, and a third approach that combines a morality based on inner freedom with structures of solidarity. In the fourth step I shall examine the premises which the three proposals provide for discourse partners on public reason and the role they accord to religion.

---

[1] H. Nagl-Docekal, *Innere Freiheit: Grenzen der nachmetaphysischen Moralkonzeptionen* (Berlin/Boston: De Gruyter, 2014), 9, 99.
[2] Cf. D. Hollenbach, *The Common Good and Christian Ethics* (Cambridge: Cambridge University Press, 2002), 149-170.

Conceptions of Self and Community in Social Ethics

I shall begin with the Aristotelian tradition, based on the polis community and two further factors. Secondly, I will outline how the individual appears as the centre of the contract approach which replaces the social bond of the previous model, community, by the social contract. The third conception presented begins with a factor which is downplayed in the first two models: the inner freedom of the human person which enables a universalist framework to be reached. A question posed to each will be how they relate to religion: as a historical and empirical reality that cannot be ignored in anthropology, social philosophy, political science and ethics? As long-standing, coherent traditions they are a factor to be reckoned with. However, if they can only be seen from the outside and compared by external criteria, they remain basically incomprehensible. Only if the concept of religion can be analysed as linked to human reason and freedom, do the historical religions become justifiable practical options, that is, reflected self-understandings chosen in the face of alternative comprehensive orientations. In order to be a dialogue partner for others in the public sphere, religions need to be understood as "not *a priori* irrational".[3] They are then seen not only as undeniable cultural factors but as having an internal connection to reason that can be analysed in a theory of self. This dimension cannot be captured with the methods of disciplines such as empirical cultural

---

[3] J. Habermas, *Between Naturalism and Religion: Philosophical Essays* (Cambridge: Polity, 2008), 112.

studies, history and law, but needs a philosophical method, which the third model of ethics, "inner freedom", provides. Having compared the three schools of ethics, the fourth part will assess how the philosophical approaches of John Rawls, Jürgen Habermas and Paul Ricoeur envisage, encourage, and set parameters for contributions from religions to the public realm.

1. *The First Framework: The Aristotelian Community Bond*

This approach anchors the practical reason and agency of the individual members in the community. Also in its modern, neo-Aristotelian form it minimises the difference between the polis and its participants. Religion does not play a constitutive role, but the model can, of course, be transferred to groups centred around the organising core of a religion. The community itself does not have to be static or oriented towards its historical foundation, but it is marked by "insiders' reasoning", as the British Kantian philosopher Onora O'Neill observes,[4] and it reflects on the values of its existing ethos in an internal, hermeneutical understanding of ethics.[5] This model is characterised by three core components that are held together in some

---

[4] O. O'Neill, *Towards Justice and Virtue: A Constructive Account of Practical Reasoning* (Cambridge: Cambridge University Press, 1996), 53.
[5] H. Schnädelbach, *Zur Rehabilitierung des 'animal rationale'* (Frankfurt a.M.: Suhrkamp, 1992), 221–222.

balance at first, but eventually unhinged through their development after antiquity.

The three elements that the German philosopher Ludwig Siep identifies as basic, also for the natural law tradition within this system, are: (1) a teleological order; (2) a polis setting; and (3) the internal dimension of conscience.[6] First, the teleological system assumed all its participants to be directed towards inbuilt goals. Secondly, corresponding to the polis setting was the understanding of the human being as a *zoon politikon*; this introduced a historical consciousness arising from dealing with the contingencies of praxis and of diverse agents, requiring a prudential use of reason. Thirdly, the internal dimension of reflection, specified further into the personal capability of conscience, could still operate within an encompassing natural order and within the parameters of a community. Yet keeping these three factors together in a productive tension was already an achievement in view of the divergent dynamics of each. Modifications in one affected the connection with the others. Siep points out how (1) teleology yields to a mechanic-technological theory of development, and finally to evolution; (2) the historical experience of cultural contingency remains, but the limits of the

---

[6] Cf. L. Siep, "Natural Law and Bioethics", in L.S. Cahill/H. Haker/E. Messi Metogo (ed.), *Human Nature and Natural Law* (London: SCM, 2010) 44–67, on p. 50. Thus, "from the start they contained a certain tension that became more acute in the modern era" (on p. 47). I am drawing on my use of his analysis in M. Junker-Kenny, *Approaches to Theological Ethics: Sources, Traditions, Visions* (London: T&T Clark, 2019).

polis are superseded; (3) the autonomy of the individual runs counter to a predetermined natural, legal or rational order.[7] The intellectual factors that held the "nurturing community" together disintegrate, and other motifs, already present in antiquity, and reinforced by biblical monotheism, such as inner freedom,[8] reappear. However, before elucidating this starting point in the third section, the framework situated at the opposite end of the spectrum has to be investigated.

2. The Contract Approach: Centred on the Individual Rational Agent

Moving from the axial age to which Aristotle belonged, to the eighteenth century in which Jean-Jacques Rousseau writes and its history of reception, crucial changes occur for the key philosophical terms of social organisation.

(1) The social bond of the polis model is replaced by the social contract; legal rules attain priority over virtues. The contract creates a framework for individuals *ex nihilo*, without social or historical links that are prior to the process of legal agreement. Not dependent on any

---

[7] Siep, "Natural Law and Bioethics", 47, 50.
[8] Cf. T. Kobusch, *Christliche Philosophie: die Entdeckung der Subjektivität* (Darmstadt: Wissenschaftliche Buchgesellschaft, 2006).

"pre-political foundations",⁹ the contract is seen as the origin of the social framework.¹⁰

(2) Prudential decisions of practical wisdom (*phronesis*) become self-interested cleverness; rational, for example in the renewed contract argumentation of John Rawls, means purposive, instrumental reason (*Verstand, Zweckrationalität*), not *Vernunft*. In Kant, *Vernunft* had been defined by its outreach towards the unconditioned, that is, its capacity to ask questions beyond the realm of what can be negotiated, to what is not at our disposition.

(3) The contract model understands the social aspect of human life as a legal framework of strict reciprocity, which is based on a *do ut des*. Yet it provides an important gain in freedom: the sphere of mere legality, of keeping to external rules, where no inner consent is needed.¹¹ Compared with the possible "tyranny of virtues" in communities where

---

⁹ For the text of 1964, "Die Entstehung des Staates als Vorgang der Säkularisation", which is at the basis also of the debate between Habermas and the then Cardinal Joseph Ratzinger, cf. E.-W. Böckenförde, *Staat, Gesellschaft, Freiheit: Studien zur Staatstheorie und zum Verfassungsrecht* (Frankfurt a.M.: Suhrkamp, 1976), 42–64.

¹⁰ Cf. P. Ricoeur, *Reflections on the Just* (Chicago: University of Chicago Press, 2007), on the "juridical tradition of the social contract" (on p. 138) which is "ahistorical" (on p. 103). Ricoeur concludes his comparison of models of the legitimation of authority with one that "admit[s] a multiple foundation, a diversity of religious and secular, rational and Romantic traditions, that mutually recognize one another as cofoundational" (on p. 105).

¹¹ Schnädelbach, *Zur Rehabilitierung des 'animal rationale'*, 228.

members have to agree to the given meanings, this aspect is seen as liberating.

(4) Neither religion nor moral conscience are required within this framework, which does without the internal, reflective dimension of the self. However, it is combinable with the expected returns of a prosperity religion and also with the concept of an electing and condemning God since external sanctions are within the realm of what can be understood.

(5) Regarding the moral foundations of democracy, the consequences of this approach have been critiqued by proponents of more demanding concepts of citizenship. A strong warning is expressed by the critical social theorist and discourse ethicist Jürgen Habermas. He regards the "democratic bond" as being under threat of "corrosion" by markets "assuming regulatory functions in domains of life that used to be held together by norms – in other words, by political means or through pre-political forms of communication",[12] as, for example, in a pluralistic democracy or in the community model. If the category of contract prevails, processes of social recognition are undermined. In a much-quoted sentence, he refers to the "paradox" formulated by the constitutional lawyer and later Supreme Court judge Ernst-Wolfgang Böckenförde that the "pacified, secular state is reliant on normative

---

[12] Habermas, *Between Naturalism and Religion*, 107–108.

presuppositions that it cannot itself guarantee";[13] Habermas anticipates that

> an uncontrolled [entgleisende] modernization of society could [...] undermine the form of solidarity on which the democratic state depends even though it cannot enforce it. Then the very constellation that Böckenförde has in mind would transpire, namely, the transformation of the citizens of prosperous and peaceful liberal societies into isolated, self-interested monads who use their individual liberties exclusively against one another like weapons.[14]

The paradox consists in the following constellation: on the one hand, the neutrality of the state was realised for reasons of principle, to protect the freedoms of religion and worldview; state neutrality and religious freedom are two sides of the same medal. Yet, on the other hand, this act of respect for individual freedom is also a risk because the state has made itself dependent on the vitality of the moral sources that feed self-understandings in civil society. These pre-political (and pre-contract) foundations have to deliver imaginative, conceptual and motivational resources that support the ability to live together.

---

[13] E.-W. Böckenförde, *Recht, Staat, Freiheit: Studien zur Rechtsphilosophie, Staatstheorie und Verfassungsgeschichte* (Frankfurt a.M.: Suhrkamp, 1991), 112, cited in Habermas, *Between Naturalism and Religion*, 111.
[14] Habermas, *Between Naturalism and Religion*, 107.

Hence a choice is emerging between creating "isolated, self-interested monads who use their individual liberties exclusively against one another like weapons" on the one side, and an understanding of individual selfhood that includes a moral, not just a legal relationship to fellow-citizens and fellow-humans, on the other.

3. Inner Freedom, Morality and Solidarity: A Universalist Approach

The Austrian philosopher Herta Nagl-Docekal observes that in contemporary philosophical ethics, morality is increasingly being replaced by a logic of contract, thus by the second model. Yet when the term 'autonomy' is used to cover actions both from self-interest and from morality, the question arises "whether this does not indicate a moral emptying of the subject".[15] Moreover, seeking the entry point to ethics in the external conditions of law has consequences for how faith traditions are seen: "Losing the inner dimension of morality out of sight results in an equal failure to illuminate the possible link between morality and religious faith".[16] A contract is self-sufficient and has no connection to prior social relationships nor to religion. A different concept of agency, self-reflection and freedom is needed: autonomy as self-legislation

---

[15] Nagl-Docekal, *Innere Freiheit*, 10.
[16] Ibid., 11.

that respects the other, "whether or not he finds them lovable";[17] it is being solidaric with people oppressed or in need since it attends to the rights and the happiness of others. Kant's understanding of autonomy as self-legislation is based on good will as a basic endowment of humans. It is the only model that has an internal connection to religion: the question of meaning (or happiness) cannot be put off for Kant, and hope is highlighted as central for agency. The postulate of the existence of God is the response to the antinomy or contradiction in which practical reason finds itself between its moral intentions and the experience of their failure against indifference, hostility, and finitude.[18] Religion is seen as empowering the individual, despite the wars fought in its name, and a communal fellowship for exchange and renewal is advocated in the concept of an ethical commonwealth provided by religious traditions.

Historically, faith communities have displayed their capability for self-reflection and transformation through the ages. Nagl-Docekal points out that religious traditions "can only persist through centuries if the believers manage – over and over again – to re-interpret the core convictions

---

[17] Everyone has a "duty to others of adopting the maxim of benevolence (practical love of man) whether or not he finds them lovable"; I. Kant, *The Doctrine of Virtue. Part II of the Metaphysic of Morals* (New York: Harper & Row, 1964), 118, cited in Nagl-Docekal, *Innere Freiheit*, 98.

[18] For a more detailed discussion, see M. Junker-Kenny, "What Scope for Ethics in the Public Sphere? Principled Autonomy and the Antinomy of Practical Reason", *Studies in Christian Ethics* 32, 4 (2019) 485–498.

of their faith in a way that renders them accessible, and convincing, in view of their respective contemporary condition".[19] The question to the three theorists of "public reason" and the "public sphere" to be treated in the next section – Rawls (1), Habermas (2) and Ricoeur (3) – is whether their concepts of religion reflect the internal capability for transformation which these traditions have shown.

4. Which Concept of Religion, Which Concept of Public Reason?

(1) The contract approach does not need religion in the sense of faith in a God who is distinct from humans and the world; it might include 'civil religion', but this use would empty the concept of religion since we would be worshipping ourselves. In John Rawls' *A Theory of Justice* (1971),[20] religion hardly plays a role. However, in the context of discovering pluralism as a lasting feature, the reality of faith traditions is included in *Political Liberalism* (1993):[21] religions and worldviews are 'comprehensive

---

[19] H. Nagl-Docekal, "'Many Forms of Non-Public Reason'? Religious Diversity in Liberal Democracies", in H. Lenk (ed.), *Comparative and Intercultural Philosophy: Proceedings of the IIP Conference, Seoul, 2008* (Münster: LIT, 2009) 79–92, on p. 85.

[20] J. Rawls, *A Theory of Justice* (Cambridge, MA: Harvard University Press, 1971).

[21] J. Rawls, *Political Liberalism* (New York: Columbia University Press, 1993).

doctrines'. Rawls's work has elements of all three frameworks distinguished here. 'Comprehensive' is close to the polis model; yet between the different communities in modern society there is no 'public' exchange, only in the 'non-public' background culture. In *A Theory of Justice*, Rawls combines an anthropology of rational choice within the renewed contract model (as well as a second foundation in 'considered convictions') with the device of the 'veil of ignorance' which secures the impartiality, or the lack of self-centredness, of the universalist deontological model, the third approach depicted here. *Political Liberalism* states that, at most, an 'overlapping consensus' can be achieved: from the observer's view from above, areas of overlap can be identified, but the reasons differ, and it only amounts to a minimalist agreement. Among the many critics that this is not sufficient or ambitious enough, the Chicago feminist theological ethicist Cristina Traina offers an instructive image: instead of a "Venn diagram: two intersecting circles", the awareness of one's "standpoint" needs to be included, in order to gain

> three dimensions rather than two. The slightest difference in experience produces a complete reorientation of perspective. Because we now see our 'common' elements from entirely different angles, each of us arrays and interprets them differently.[22]

---

[22] C.L.H. Traina, *Feminist Ethics and Natural Law: The End of the Anathemas* (Washington, DC: Georgetown University Press, 1999), 3.

Only by moving to the participants' perspective, can the real, glittering pluralism be made visible. All the facets from different contexts matter, when different players agree, for example, on the need for ecological protection. Are we motivated to protect the biosphere because we are part of nature? Or because it is a matter of being stewards for God's creation? Or due to the earth being our Pachamama? All these facets from different origins play a role when negotiators from across the world agree on limits, as at the Paris climate accord in 2015.

(2) For Habermas, the contribution of religious traditions to re-energising the social bond and a normative consciousness lie in the heuristic and motivating capacities that their world-disclosing language makes available:

> Pure practical reason can no longer be so confident in its ability to counteract a modernization spinning out of control armed solely with the insights of a theory of justice. The latter lacks the creativity of linguistic world-disclosure that a normative consciousness afflicted with accelerating decline requires in order to regenerate itself.[23]

All resources of meaning are needed, translations are possible, and comprehensive doctrines are not towers in the landscape like Bologna's impressive *torri pendenti*, the Asinelli and the Garisenda towers; instead, all traditions of

---

[23] Habermas, *Between Naturalism and Religion*, 211.

interpretation are part of a forum where citizens speak to each other, both in the modes of "creative world-disclosure" and of discourse on what is universalisable and can thus be adopted as justified for all affected.

(3) The French hermeneutical philosopher Paul Ricoeur sees religions as 'co-founders' of the public sphere. They have symbolic and practical legacies in it and an interest to participate in the project of "living well, with and for others, in just institutions".[24] He urges Christian communities to take up, "without any hang-ups, their part in this co-foundation in open competition with other, heterogeneous traditions, which themselves are reinvigorated and driven by their unkept promises".[25]

With this point which the others do not consider, Ricoeur adds the internal perspective and motivation of believers. They owe it to their tradition to actualise its unspent potential today in dynamic and praxis-oriented ways. For Ricoeur, this is possible due to the "logics of superabundance" that marks the biblical texts. The presupposition for an understanding of public reason that is driven by its unkept promises is a thinking of plenitude; it differs from Rawls' carefully balanced reciprocity as a stability-producing context, and equally from Habermas' perceptiveness about processes of modernisation that have run out of control.

---

[24] P. Ricoeur, *Oneself as Another* (Chicago: University of Chicago Press, 1992), 172.
[25] Ricoeur, *Reflections on the Just*, 105.

5. Conclusion

From these different starting points, the question whether religions are to be regarded as irritants, as counter-agents, as mediators, or as competitors for public reason can only be indicated but not answered. What should be clear, however, is that comprehensive doctrines, among them religions, are examples of the good only in a formal sense. It is a matter of moral examination whether they are good also in their content, or whether they are dismissive of other communities, coercive or reductionist.[26] Habermas has established three criteria for religious traditions: the ability and willingness (1) to recognise the distinction between secular and religious authority; (2) to allow for the autonomy of the sciences and humanities; and (3) to accept the existence of other religions.[27] But the secular side is equally afflicted with tendencies that need to be corrected: above all the reduction of morality to law, and of respect for the other even when it is not reciprocated to self-interested, "prudential" caution. The symbolic worlds of the religions, the chain of memory, the backdrop of the cosmos or the universe have the potential to break up a security-driven, suspicious and cynical view of the other. As the systematic theologian Margit Eckholt sums up

---

[26] C. Hübenthal, *Grundlegung der christlichen Sozialethik: Versuch eines freiheitsanalytisch-handlungsreflexiven Ansatzes* (Münster: Aschendorff, 2006), 368.

[27] Habermas, *Between Naturalism and Religion*, 137.

Ricoeur's conclusions of his "Reflections on a New Ethos for Europe": they can contribute from their own depth to the task of combining "translation, exchange of cultural memory and reconciliation as models of intercultural hermeneutics"; by "setting free the memory of the unkept promises of the past", they can generate a new creativity to carry forward the as yet "incomplete future of the past".[28]

---

[28] M. Eckholt, "Übersetzung, Erinnerung, Versöhnung: Frauen in Europa auf der Suche nach Gestalten einer verbindenden Spiritualität", in P. Hünermann/J. Juhant/B. Žalec (ed.), *Dialogue and Virtue: Ways to Overcome Clashes of Our Civilization* (Münster: LIT, 2007) 57–68, on p. 60.

Individuals and Communities: What Did Jewish Contemporary Thought Bring to Political Theory?
Sophie Nordmann

Over the past century, there have been many intense conversations in the sphere of political philosophy. These conversations mostly addressed modern forms of social and political organisation, such as liberal democracy, totalitarianism and socialism since the tragic historical experiences of the past century also raised many questions for it. Among other circumstances, two world wars and the rise of totalitarian regimes induced philosophers to rethink anew how individuals are part of civil society, how civil society and the state are connected, and how a single political community may encompass various social, cultural, and religious communities.

Jewish thinkers were at the forefront of some of these discussions. In a sense, they had to give priority to these major questions, addressing them with a particular intensity, because they affected the Jewish world as they knew it in a specific way. One illustration of this point is the question of the creation of a Jewish state in Palestine, which goes back to the late nineteenth century and the emergence of political Zionism. This issue led to intense debates among German-Jewish thinkers, long before other movements of national liberation of the twentieth century, during decolonisation or after the fall of the Soviet Union, raised the issue of political sovereignty on a global scale. A second illustration of this point is the debates that made Mandatory Palestine (1920–1948) and the newly independent state of Israel into an extraordinary laboratory of various forms of community organisations, most emblematically the kibbutz. Finally, the minority situation of the Jewish diaspora in Europe and the United States led Jewish thinkers to discuss the status of cultural and religious minorities, an issue central to contemporary political theory. What is at stake in all these discussions is the question of individuals and of their membership in communities of different types, whether interconnected or competing.

1. Religious Membership and Political Citizenship

The Zionist project of creating a Jewish state in Palestine raised vocal debates within the Jewish intellectual world at the beginning of the twentieth century. The key question was whether a religious community could become a political community. As is well known, Zionism as a political project was a recent idea at the time. Although Theodor Herzl was its best-known flag bearer, there was actually not one but many different Zionisms, all resulting from the collapse of the traditional structures of Jewish life, the growth of modern nationalism and the strength of anti-Semitism as exemplified by the pogroms in Eastern Europe, the rise of anti-Semitism in Imperial Germany, and the Dreyfus Affair in France.

Less known is the fact that Zionism encountered strong opposition within the intellectual and philosophical Jewish world at the time. One of the most famous Jewish opponents to Zionism at the beginning of the twentieth century was Hermann Cohen (1842–1918), then an emeritus professor at the University of Marburg and at the Academy of Jewish Sciences in Berlin. He was one of the most distinguished philosophers of his time in the tradition of Immanuel Kant and he was also an authority in the German Jewish intellectual community. His firm opposition to Zionism was grounded in two political and philosophical arguments. First, he envisioned Judaism as universal and therefore impossible to constrict within national boundaries. Second, his political philosophy, particularly his conception of what a political community should be and what role the state should play, led him to oppose Zionism. In his view, Zionist aspirations to political sovereignty resulted from a serious confusion between cultural membership and political citizenship that was unfortunately frequent in that era of nationalism. Since the mid-nineteenth century, he lamented, there had been an inflation of political demands under the influence of Romantic ideas that emphasised connections between individuals and a particular language, culture, or religion. Every community, including that of the Jews, wanted its own political state: according to Cohen, the growth of political Zionism resulted from this inflation of nationalism.

In his view, such a demand was mistaken. To belong to a specific cultural and religious community and to belong to a political community were two very different things. Membership in a particular community sets individuals apart and makes them different from other individuals belonging to other particular communities. On the other hand, membership in a political community brings individuals together and makes them all citizens, i.e. identical and equal, no matter to which particular community they also belong. In a state of law, all citizens are equal as citizens. This is a founding principle of the state of law. Therefore, to confuse the two types of membership is to undermine the foundations of the state of law and of the political community. It represents a profound misunderstanding of the goal of the political community, which is precisely to weave together a plurality of communities into one political unit.

For each particular community to claim political sovereignty for itself would be akin to signing the end of politics, as the vocation of a political community is not to embody a particular cultural or religious community but to allow for the coexistence of different communities within a single political unit. Therefore, the fact of being a member of the Jewish community and the fact of being a citizen of a state (in Cohen's case, Germany) are two facts of different yet fully compatible orders. There is no need for Jews to have their own state: such a demand is only the result of a confusion between membership in a religious community and membership in a political community. Therefore, the Zionist programme of a Jewish state is, in

Cohen's words, "an insult to the patriotic feelings of those Jews who find a national foyer in the country where they live".[1]

Hermann Cohen's argument raised strong protests in the Jewish intellectual world. Among others, Martin Buber engaged in a vigorous debate with Cohen. According to him, Cohen lost himself in theoretical considerations that had little to do with reality. The reality was that Jewish men and women lived under oppression and constant threats. It gave legitimacy to Jewish aspirations to political sovereignty, which was the only way for Jews to cease to be dependent. These debates signalled different visions of the nature and of the role of political communities. Zionism prompted Hermann Cohen, Martin Buber and many other Jewish thinkers to deal with these issues in an avant-garde fashion, decades before decolonisation and the fall of the Soviet Union raised them on a global scale.

---

[1] H. Cohen, *Jüdische Schriften*, ed. B. Strauss (3 vol.; Berlin: Schwetschke, 1924), 216 (my translation). On this, see e.g. J.A. Barash, "Politics and Theology: The Debate on Zionism between Hermann Cohen and Martin Buber", in P. Mendes-Flohr (ed.), *Dialogue as a Trans-Disciplinary Concept: Martin Buber's Philosophy of Dialogue and Its Contemporary Reception* (Berlin: De Gruyter, 2015) 49–60; S. Nordmann, "Hermann Cohen et le sionisme", *Revue d'études germaniques* 2 (2004) 327–342; S. Nordmann, "Germanisme, judaïsme, sionisme: portraits croisés", in M.-A. Lescourret (dir.), *La dette et la distance: de quelques élèves et lecteurs juifs de Heidegger* (Paris: Éditions de l'éclat, 2014) 205–221.

2. Modern Atomised Society and Human Community

Martin Buber's criticism of modern society and his alternative vision of a living community provides a second case in point. Buber (1878–1965) was born into an assimilated Jewish family in Vienna in 1878 and he went on to study philosophy and art history. He published many texts on Judaism, particularly on Hasidism, and a philosophical essay untitled *Ich und Du* published in 1923.[2] He taught Jewish religious philosophy at the University of Frankfurt during the 1920s and 1930s. He left Germany in 1938 and became a professor at the Hebrew University of Jerusalem. Until his death in 1965, he was active in Israel's political and social debates.[3]

Buber's Zionist engagement resulted from his strong criticism of the modern state and modern society. According to him, the modern world is a nightmare in which individuals lose all sense of reality and entertain no living relationship with themselves and those around them. The modern world is impersonal, disembodied, and managed by causality. In the economic sphere, individuals form an anonymous workforce. In the political sphere, individuals are abstract citizens. Anyone can replace anyone. Everyone is merely a pawn or a number. According to modern

---

[2] M. Buber, *Ich und Du* (Leipzig: Insel-Verl., 1923); ET: *I and Thou* (Edinburgh: T&T Clark, 1937).
[3] On this, see e.g. D. Bourel, *Martin Buber: sentinelle de l'humanité* (Paris: Albin Michel, 2015).

science, men are the result of a determinist biological evolution and a determinist historical evolution. The lives of their minds are regulated by determinist, objective and impersonal laws. Mechanisation, rationalisation, objectivity, depersonalisation, bureaucratisation, chains, processes and laws reign supreme. In Buber's view, the modern world is a dead world, devoid of any living being. Individuals are only the ghosts of themselves. This nightmare is what Buber called the triumph of the 'that'.

Central in this nightmarish world is the role played by economics (modern capitalism) and politics (the modern state). Modern capitalism, chain work, assembly lines and general competition destroyed the economic structures of living human communities. The central state also weakened particular human communities: "Thereafter centralism in its new, capitalistic form succeeded where the old had failed: in atomizing society".[4] Capitalism only wants to tackle individuals and dominates them with machines, and the modern state makes this easier by making groups weaker and less autonomous. The result of this process is the loss of what Buber calls "the most valuable of all goods – the life between man and man".[5] Lacking these lively relations, autonomy loses its meaning, personal relationships dry up: "The personal human being ceases to be the living member of a social body and becomes a cog in the

---

[4] M. Buber, *Paths in Utopia* (Boston: Beacon Press, 1958), 139.
[5] Ibid., 132.

'collective' machine".⁶ In the world of capitalism and the central state, individuals are only numerical and impersonal units who have no real relationship with other individuals and do not belong to a living human community.

In his writings, Buber calls upon men to wake up from this nightmare. Waking up means realising that another world is possible. Instead of an aggregation of individuals and the atomisation of society, there would be a world of relationships and presence where each individual is connected to others in the midst of a living organic community. Clearly, in making such an argument, Buber echoes the famed distinction between *Gemeinschaft* and *Gesellschaft* suggested by his contemporary Ferdinand Tönnies. Buber's living community, however, is not inspired by Tönnies nor by the German Romantic thinkers who looked back nostalgically at the communities in a lost (and fictional) Golden Age. As the philosopher Michael Löwy suggests, Buber's inspiration is not pre-modern; he does not look back at European medieval corporations or guilds as models.⁷ In his article "Alte und neue Gemeinschaft", Buber wrote: "We can certainly not back away from mechanised society but we can go beyond it towards a new organicism".⁸ He draws his ideas of "a new organicism" from

---

⁶ Ibid.
⁷ M. Löwy, "Messianisme et utopie", *Cités* 42 (2010) 33-40, on p. 36; M. Löwy, *Rédemption et utopie: le judaïsme libertaire en Europe centrale* (Paris: Presses Universitaires de France, 1988), 63-64.
⁸ M. Buber, "Alte und neue Gemeinschaft" (1900), published by P. Mendes-Flohr/B. Susser, "*Alte und neue Gemeinschaft*: An Unpublished Buber

the Jewish world and particularly from the Hasidic communities of Galicia, which he visited as a child with his grandfather. Hasidism is a Jewish mystical movement that appeared in Eastern Europe in the late eighteenth century. It is based on ideas drawn from the Kabbalah and the notion of a divine presence everywhere in the world and in each and every action of daily life. Members are organised into relatively small communities gathered around a master, the Tsaddik.

Buber wrote many vibrant descriptions of life in Hasidic communities, not long before the tragedies of the twentieth century erased them forever. These communities inspired him to envision a world where individuals would be truly alive and embodied within an organic community, to which they would belong on the mode of the 'you' and not of the 'that'. While Buber did not intend to convert his contemporaries to Hasidism and never joined a Hasidic community himself, he saw in Hasidism possibilities for the future, that is, elements of an alternative model of human organisation, in which individuals and communities would not disappear.

Surprising as it may seem, Buber's criticism of the modern society and his analysis of Hasidic communities led him to socialism. His discussions of works by Pierre-Joseph Proudhon, Henri de Saint-Simon, Peter Kropotkin, Karl Marx and Vladimir Lenin aimed at clearing the way

---

Manuscript", *AJS Review* 1 (1976) 41–56, cited in Löwy, *Rédemption et utopie*, 65 (my translation).

towards a new socialism. Indeed, the arrival of Zionist Jews in Palestine became an extraordinary laboratory for the communities Buber called for. Buber directly inspired one of the Zionist realisations of the time, the kibbutzim – the farming villages created by Zionist pioneers during the first half of the twentieth century. Many of their founders read Buber or had been his students. Community members held in common the means of production as well as wealth. There was no circulation of money nor were there salaries. Community life dictated the assignment of tasks; collective life set the rhythm for individual lives; village members voted on daily matters requiring collective decisions. Despite their flaws and limits, the kibbutzim offered concrete examples of human communities where members all knew each other, where an organic relationship connected the community and its individual members, and where individuals were fully engaged in a relationship with each other.

In the course of time, kibbutzim changed and did not escape capitalism and political centralisation. In comparison with all other attempts at building socialism, however, these villages remained for Buber a unique example of a socialist community that did not fail. "As I see history and the present", he wrote,

> there is only one all-out effort to create a Full Co-operative which justifies our speaking of success in the socialistic sense, and that is the Jewish Village Commune in its various forms, as found in Palestine. [...] Thus on the soberest survey and on the soberest reflection one can

say that, in this one spot in a world of partial failures, we can recognize a non-failure – and, such as it is, a signal non-failure.[9]

In Buber's view, therefore, Hasidic communities and kibbutzim embody two models of the community constituted by real relationships between individuals who fully live their individual lives in the community and through the community. If Buber's thoughts on the individual and the community are indeed rooted in the Jewish experience, it may seem surprising that he chose two models that appear so completely opposed. Hasidic communities are religious communities, traditionally minded, and entirely devoted to the experience of mysticism in daily life. Kibbutzim, on the other hand, are lay, socialist, religion-free farming communities which develop a communitarian organisation in order to survive in their natural environment. Between these two models, however, there is in fact a very strong connection. First, there is a link between Jewish religious traditions and socialist aspirations. In Buber's view, the Jewish tradition is, along with Plato's philosophy, one of the sources of socialism. The prophets were the first to affirm the desire "of a purer, nicer, truer common life and of an authentic human community based on love, reciprocal understanding, and mutual help".[10] Second, Hasidic

---

[9] Buber, *Paths in Utopia*, 141–142.
[10] M. Buber, *Drei Reden über das Judentums* (Frankfurt a.M.: Rütten & Loening, 1920), 94 (my translation).

communities and kibbutzim shared the same idea of community. It is little known that the word 'kibbutz' was used for the first time by Hasidim to designate a human community. More precisely, the word 'kibbutz' was first used by one of the major figures of Hasidism to qualify, precisely, the community of Hasidim gathered around their Tsaddik.

A short Hasidic tale – tales being a favourite Hasidic way of passing on knowledge – illustrates the connection between Hasidic visions of community and socialist kibbutzim visions of it very well. This tale is not about nightmares and dreams, as in Buber's writings, but about something quite close: hell and paradise. It runs thus: When Moses arrives before God, God tells him: "Ask me what you want and I will give it to you". Moses says: "O Lord of the universe, I would like to see how the just are rewarded and the misbelievers live in hell". God takes Moses to stand in front of two doors. He opens the first door and tells Moses to look inside. In the centre of the room there is a huge round table. In the middle of this table is a large pot full of a deliciously smelling stew. Moses almost wants to taste it. Around the table sit men and women. They are all emaciated, livid, silent and sick, and look famished. They each hold a spoon with a very long handle that is attached to their arm. With this they can reach the stew and help themselves. However, since the spoon handle is longer than their arm, they cannot bring the spoon back to their mouth. Moses sees their misery and their suffering and he shivers. God tells him: "You just saw hell". Then God and Moses go to the second door. God opens it. Moses sees a scene that is identical to the previous one.

There is the huge roundtable. There is the pot with the delicious stew, which Moses again would like to taste. The men and women around the table are equipped with the same long-handled spoons. This time, however, the men and women around the table are well-fed, quite plump, smiling, talking to each other and laughing. God closes the door and tells Moses: "You just saw paradise". Moses says: "God, I do not understand". God says: "Have a better look". Once again he opens the door. Moses looks again and sees that all the men and women around the table put their spoon in the pot and then feed the person in front of them.

This tale could be one of the thousand tales that Martin Buber compiled in his famous 1947 anthology, *Tales of the Hasidim*.[11] It is clear that this tale is not about God and Moses but about real men and women, here and now. It is about paradise and hell on earth. The tale's hell is modern society, desiccated, atomised and constituted of individuals who are only the ghosts of themselves. The tale's paradise is Buber's human community, fully alive, consisting of relations and presences, nourishing for its members and nourished by its members. In a way, Buber transposes the Hasidic view of community in his philosophical and political thought in order to develop both his criticism of modern society and his nourishing the socialist model of communitarian organisation he is invoking.

---

[11] M. Buber, *Tales of the Hasidim* (2 vol.; New York: Schocken Books, 1947–1948).

3. Cultural and Religious Communities in the Democratic State

The question of the status of cultural minorities in contemporary liberal and democratic states such as the United States provides a third case in point. Over the last four decades, liberal thinkers who envision individuals devoid of any communitarian sense of belonging and communitarian thinkers for whom membership in specific communities define individuals have vigorously disagreed over this central issue of political philosophy and theory. What is fundamentally at stake in this debate is the relationship of the individual to the community. In this respect there is one key difference between liberals and communitarians. Liberal thinkers argue that the accomplishment of an individual requires his/her emancipation from the communities to which s/he belongs. The function of politics, in their view, is to provide individuals with the means of this emancipation. On the contrary, communitarians argue that the accomplishment of an individual requires his/her membership in one or several communities. These communities, moreover, must be as vital as possible in order for individuals to develop fully therein. In their view, political authorities must not coerce communities but be sufficiently supple and protective to allow for their full growth.

One of the major participants in this debate is the Jewish-American thinker Michael Walzer (1935–). As a philosopher and political theorist, Walzer was active in the American civil rights movement of the 1960s. In reaction to John

Rawls' milestone *A Theory of Justice* (1971),[12] he developed an alternative conception of justice, which was expressed in his 1983 book, *Spheres of Justice*.[13] In this work, Walzer opened a new path in the debate between liberals and communitarians. This path is rooted in Jewish thought and in the individual, family and historical Jewish experience of having belonged to a minority community for centuries. Walzer starts from the awareness that the existence of communities is an anthropological fact, which persists under any type of political regime, whether empires, monarchies, democratic nation-states or totalitarianism. Political regimes may change but the fact remains that individuals continue to belong to, or join, groups that have their own history, culture and identity. History shows that it is possible to repress a cultural community, whether violently or gently, but not to suppress it. Walzer uses the examples of the contemporary resurgence of communitarian demands in Western liberal states. He also argues that in communist regimes cultural and religious communities suffered decades of oppression but survived, even forcefully re-emerging, after the fall of these regimes. In a famous article, Walzer calls this phenomenon a "new tribalism".[14] He concludes that tribes reappear more forcefully

---

[12] J. Rawls, *A Theory of Justice* (Cambridge, MA: Harvard University Press, 1971).

[13] M. Walzer, *Spheres of Justice: A Defense of Pluralism and Equality* (New York: Basic Books, 1983).

[14] M. Walzer, "The New Tribalism: Notes on a Difficult Problem", *Dissent* (Spring 1992) 164-171.

where they have been most severely repressed. Individuals belong to communities, and it is impossible to escape this anthropological fact.

Furthermore, in Walzer's view, community membership does not prevent political and social unity. On the contrary, far from opposing each other, community membership and political citizenship nourish each other. The more active the communities of all types, the easier it is for an individual to become involved in diverse particular memberships as well as political citizenship. In countries where cultural communities are tolerated or encouraged, such as Australia, Canada and the United States, many cultural militants broaden their horizon and become involved in a great number of local and national causes. On the contrary, where community membership is denied, strategies of resistance develop along with a tendency to communitarian confinement. In the case of the United States, for instance, Walzer argues that it is often among Native Americans and African Americans, the two groups that historically suffered from the greatest lack of recognition, that numerous individuals break off community membership and do not pursue a trajectory of positive individual affirmation. Instead, they experience dire cultural and economic circumstances that marginalise them even further.

Community membership, thus, does not prevent national membership. On the contrary, community membership is an important vector of national membership. As Walzer argues, communities are schools of citizenship. Publically interested citizens come from groups that teach them the notion that their individual interest is connected to the interest of the whole group. In Walzer's view, the development of community membership, whether cultural, religious, local, trade unionist, etc., is an absolute necessity. It is therefore in the state's best general interest to create conditions that will favour the development of an egalitarian community.

Walzer's conception differs both from the communitarian view, which would have community membership supersede national civic membership, and from the liberal view, which would delegitimise cultural communities. His pluralist model stems from his experience as a member of the Jewish-American community. He claims to express himself with both a Jewish and an American voice, a twentieth-century voice, a male voice, a white voice, etc., and he claims to do so based on his connection to a historical tradition and a particular experience. In this conception, the Jewish community experience is central. Noting that his grandparents fled tsarist oppression and settled in the United States, Walzer argues that this particular experience explains why many Jewish thinkers, himself included, choose to focus on the question of social justice and on the recognition of cultural and religious minorities.

Walzer is also an heir to Jewish thinkers of the Eastern Europe diaspora. At the beginning of the twentieth century, Eastern European Jewish thinkers faced the precarious situation of all Jewish diaspora communities, and they discussed the way in which Jewish communities might maintain their collective character in their host countries. Walzer's cultural pluralism and his emphasis on active civic involvement as a natural consequence of community involvement echo these reflections. As the French sociologist Simon Wuhl suggests, there is a link between Walzer's cultural pluralism and the ideas of the Eastern European Jewish historian Simon Dubnow. Dubnow was particularly interested in the perennial survival of diasporic Judaism, and he vigorously argued that Jewish integration into host societies should be based on equal rights in the political sphere and on the recognition of their collective personality in the cultural sphere. Dubnow was convinced that the recognition of the Jewish diaspora as a cultural entity, far from being an obstacle, was a necessary condition for their full acceptance of the host nation. Walzer inherited this Jewish political and philosophical tradition and adapted it to the specific problems of his time and his country. He constitutes, therefore, another example of the way in which Jewish thought feeds a thinker's views about individuals and their communities of membership.[15]

Two main reasons account for the choice of the three case studies discussed above. One is chronological and geographical. Hermann Cohen's opposition to political Zionism took place in the early twentieth century. Martin Buber developed both his criticism of modern society and his vision of what he called the true community between the 1920s and the 1950s. Michael Walzer entered the debate between liberals and communitarians and offered

---

[15] S. Wuhl, *Michael Walzer et l'empreinte du judaïsme* (Lormont: Le Bord de l'eau, 2017).

his views on cultural pluralism during the 1970s and the 2000s. Cohen, Buber, and Walzer take the reader from Central and Eastern Europe to Israel and to the United States. With them we cross time and move in space. Second, at stake in the debate on Zionism is the question of the nature and the finality of the political community; in Buber's political theory, it is a question of the insertion of the individual into a true, lively community; in Walzer's discussion of cultural pluralism, it is the question of the articulation between cultural communities and the political community. References to Jewish sources and traditions, moreover, nourish their thoughts on these central questions of contemporary social and political theory.

In Search of a Contemporary Sharī'a Discourse of Pluralism
Tim Winter

One of early modern history's most iconic confrontations between traditional and Enlightenment forms of life arose when Napoleon Bonaparte occupied the ancient city of Cairo, following his crushing defeat of the archaically equipped Mamluk forces on 21 July 1798. In this paradigmatic Eastern place, he found an urban and societal metabolism radically alien to the unitary Enlightenment perfectionism espoused by the scientists and philosophers who accompanied his army and who adumbrated his vision for improving the world. Lacking a central square or forum, or even a supreme place of worship, Cairo presented an agglutinative labyrinth of alleyways and canals; arteries without a heart. The largest visible module was the *hāra*, the quarter, a kind of parish centred on a mosque, a church or a synagogue; and yet little seemed to knit these parishes together. Frenchmen who ventured within a *hāra* found a claustrophobically intimate and curiously self-regulating commune, where families disputed and intermarried, and appointed their own magistrates, night-watchmen and religious personnel. The ruler was acknowledged in sermons and in inscriptions on coins, but in practice seemed to exert only a slight influence on life. Society in these autonomous neighbourhood universes was shaped by duty, not individual freedom or the *droits de l'homme*: the duty to marry, to have children, to serve in a guild, to pray as one's ancestors had always prayed. The master-signifier was not the enlightened polity, but God.

To the rational encyclopaedists who escorted the army of occupation this decentralised arrangement seemed to be not only a denial of progress but also a security risk. Shortly after the invasion, an insurgency in those same alleyways killed three hundred French soldiers; as with Iraq and Palestine in our own times, the occupation proved as troublesome as the invasion had been easy. The Mamluk beys might be dead or dispersed, but the polycentric resilience of Muslim urban life was undiminished.

So the great gates and walls which had divided the *hāras* were demolished. The beginnings of a new, more reasonable city were laid down to the west of the old quarters. In due season, arrow-straight boulevards, *rond-points*, and civic parks rose up to become home to a plurality of lighter-skinned entrepreneurs and merchants: Greeks, Sicilians and other *khawājāt*, foreign lords. Between the two urban worlds lay the no man's land of the Azbakeya, scene of doubtful bars and brothels, home to every marginal and deracinated individual fleeing regimentation, whether of the Eastern or the Western kind. Into this *demi-monde*, as though in an attempt to knit the two halves into one, came to be planted uncompromising emblems of the burgeoning modern state: the central post office, the fire brigade, and the famous opera house at which *Aida* had its premiere.

Cairo's polarised topography, soon replicated in most metropolitan spaces across the Islamic world, represents in physical form the troubled dimorphism of modernised Muslim culture. The old city could not be simply repainted, electrified, and integrated into the European future. Its logic was illogical, for it had not been designed to be a cog in a greater machine. The society which called it home seemed at best picturesque, at worse a barbarian emblem of the Enlightenment's darkest 'other', a Semitism wallowing in a sea of laws and responsa, ordered and hierarchised neither by a saviour nor by science. In its allergy to state centralism, its ritualism, its love of privacy and of the autonomy of the extended family unit, it was Oriental unreason; it was, the biblically-minded remarked, Ishmael, the rejected, wild, Egyptian son of Abraham, whose younger and chosen brother now strolled through the elegant shopping streets to the West. It was certainly not anarchic, but it represented a socio-political order of a categorically different and strange kind, which welled up from within extended families, neighbourhoods, guilds and confessional traditions, and was hardly shaped at all by the guiding hand of government.

The repercussions of this dichotomy persist even now, two centuries later. Today the *khawājāt* are gone, ethnically cleansed by Nasser's revolution. But atop the Muqattam Hills, and in other airy hygienic places far from the decaying labyrinths, the elites remain substantively Western, even when they retain some Muslim pieties. They live in quarters called Golf City or Green Land, and the imperial tongue is likely to be the language favoured at home. Their gated communities are self-consciously and entirely Occidental in their planning and design idiom. Europe's ratio is claimed to have triumphed again in these cantonments, against the folkways which stubbornly persist in the working-class alleys which provide the servants and labourers for the new exurbs. Out of this unresolved mutual alienation, whose shaping of the city's geography is clearly visible even from the flight path into Cairo Airport, arise many of Islam's current discontents. From the time of Napoleon's violent insertion of positivist reason, modernity's project of a unified and centralised rational society has ironically unsettled and dichotomised the Muslims; and in the liminal zone between the alternate worlds the tensions produce not only prostitutes and pederasts, but, in our times, religious puritans who excoriate both universes as equally dislodged and treasonably exiled from authentic belonging.

Deep in the ruined *hāras*, thronged now with rural migrants, old habits have in some measure endured, and an indicative aspect of this is that they seem at ease with multiplicity, autonomy and antinomy. The hashish smoker still sits outside the mosque; the tombs of the prophet's kin are still the scenes of riotous and sometimes far from normative religious performances. Illiterate Muslim women light candles in a Uniate church before gathering for the ecstatic *zār* ritual in a discreet lodgement. Magic is widely practised and universally feared. Despite the disapproval both of the fundamentalists and of the enlightened

In Search of a Contemporary Sharī'a Discourse of Pluralism

Anglophones of Golf City, hints of an older Levantine diversity linger in the air, recalling a differently adjusted age of faith when charisma was locally generated and not governmentally scripted, when holiness felt more interesting than centrally controlled boundaries, and when healers and sainted wonder-workers drew more crowds than the *hadīth* expert on the radio. Charisma in these places still seeks to be routinised by the neighbourly rather than the national.

Set against this is a modernity which insists on the current unviability of the decentralised medieval *sharī'a* vision. Seyla Benhabib holds that "movements for maintaining the purity or distinctiveness of cultures seem [...] irreconcilable with both democratic and more basic epistemological considerations".[1] For modernity, deistic at best but often overtly irreligious, traditional Islam's sourcing of authority through immanent (*tashbīh*) experiences of the sacred, which naturally supports a landscape of localised and often disconnected sacralities and sources of wisdom, must be replaced by a more 'rational' emphasis on divine transcendence (*tanzīh*), or, increasingly, by the scientific disenchantment of the material world and the reduction of all the experiences of human life to expressions of the profanely physical. Science, with its love of unitary explications, is no friend to cultural diversity. Salafist fundamentalism, too, with its hostility to the localised sacred,

---

[1] S. Benhabib, *The Claims of Culture: Equality and Diversity in the Global Era* (Princeton: Princeton University Press, 2002), ix.

tries to produce singular interpretations, and habitually seeks to impose these from above.

From the Muqattam Hills arises the hortatory call to modernisation: the city is susurrated by media messages of progress, women's rights, and a centrally supplied list of repetitively vaunted freedoms. The old *hāras* cannot broadcast back; their culture, which gives their lives a distinctive and meaningful texture, is unheard by the wealthy, still less by the Western agencies which anxiously campaign for reform in these worrisome Arab places. As Lila Abu-Lughod has noted, the missiology of the international consensus – for which read Western elites – has been purely imperial, and has no time at all for the moral and human experience of the Ishmaelite and Hagarene 'other'. Feminism, for instance, looks like just another Orientalism here: the East still cannot speak for itself, and must still be saved from itself. Abu-Lughod writes this:

> I have done fieldwork in Egypt over more than 20 years, and I cannot think of a single woman I know [...] who has ever expressed envy of US women, women they tend to perceive as bereft of community, vulnerable to sexual violence and social anomie, driven by individual success rather than morality, or strangely disrespectful of God.[2]

---

[2] L. Abu-Lughod, "Do Muslim Women Really Need Saving? Anthropological Reflections on Cultural Relativism and Its Others", *American Anthropologist* 104/3 (2002) 783–790, on p. 788.

In Search of a Contemporary Sharī'a Discourse of Pluralism

In this way the wreck of medieval Muslim sociality in old Cairo continues to be the object of discursive violence by local and global elites; and its own voice, dismissed now by Salafism as well, is hardly heard or even imagined. Napoleon's *mission civilisatrice*, after two centuries still a work in progress, seems too rational and scientific to be dialogical with human subjects mired in so alien a folk consciousness, driven as it is by its insistence on the immanence of the sacred and the possibility of permanent unresolved difference. It is like the juxtaposition of an organic living thing evolved over millennia with an efficient machine; a common substance is absent. And the Islamisms sparked by the collision of the two worlds show no interest in restoring the old modular pattern of Muslim urban life, favouring the corporatism of an 'Islamic state', more often than not totalitarian in its desire to encourage or impose uniformity and to erode or persecute difference.

Let us, then, imaginatively ventriloquise for the unheard tenement dwellers, those who are unrepresented in the circle of our learned academic commentariat which ponders their identity and maps their appropriate progression. The urban poor of the *dār al-Islām*, it has been suggested, inherit the ruins of a culture which was devout but which sustainably managed resilient and distinctive forms of plurality, facilitated by a sense that holiness (*baraka*) was local as well as transcendent. The emphasis on strong self-governing families and urban districts did not merely generate and coexist with an Islamic polycentrism, but was allowed to be the matrix for non-Muslim modules as well. From a window at an al-Azhar student hostel one may still hear a Franciscan bell tolling the Angelus each morning (ironically, since Pope Callixtus III had initiated this as an anti-Muslim practice). In a deeper alleyway near the Azhar may be discovered a ruined synagogue, now an encampment for poor migrants from the Delta. Its Jews, however, have all fled. Modernity, the French Grande Armée's Enlightenment with its ideology of public religious equality and state indifference, seems to have cataclysmically reduced a diversity, both Muslim and Abrahamic, which was once a constitutive reality.

Our discussion, then, starts with this antinomy, which in a sense is a distinctive Islamic iteration of the familiar paradox of globalisation: in the name of empowering infinite choices for the individual, cultures wither and we become generic; elites, enabled by the bureaucracies of the nation-state and by privileged media access, tend to be irresistible hegemons. But in invoking the lexicon of reason and pluralism we beg the question of which rationality, whose pluralism? For pre-modern Islam, convinced of local holiness, denied neither of these things, although it found a very different mode of sourcing them. Despite a recurrent Sufi trope which taught that God would be forgiving towards mistaken dogmatic fixities,[3] in its central doctrines Muslim theology was certainly not pluralistic

---

[3] R.P. Mottahedeh, "Pluralism and Islamic Traditions of Sectarian Divisions", in Z. Hirji (ed.), *Diversity and Pluralism in Islam: Historical and Contemporary Discourses amongst Muslims* (London/New York: I.B. Tauris, 2010) 31–42.

In Search of a Contemporary Sharīʿa Discourse of Pluralism

in intention, since an elementary law of non-contradiction applies to metaphysical truth-claims. A simultaneous belief in a one-off resurrection and cyclical reincarnation, to take one instance, would clearly be incoherent. Muslim theology agrees essentially with the Orthodox Jewish observation that "if orthodoxy is true then non-orthodoxy is false. Pluralism and relativism are concepts that have no place in a religion of revelation".[4] However Islam's prophetic insistence on truth coexisted with, and ultimately guaranteed, the substantive pluralisms of the Ishmaelite socio-legal dispensation. Famously diverse and polycentric, although surely not quite so amorphous as Shahab Ahmed has suggested in a recent book,[5] this favoured a strong subsidiarity in social structures, engendering cultures and laws which naturally enabled difference and the proliferation of centres of sacral and civil authority.

How might this pre-modern multifariousness of Islam's social habits generate a plurality of a type acceptable to modern elites? Islam's fissiparous tendencies stem from ideas of the divine immanence, which can create a sacred value which appears to well up from within individuals and objects; by contrast, liberalism's tolerance of difference is centrally envisaged and enacted, resulting from an Enlightenment conviction that the state should have no

---

[4] J.D. Bleich's argument as summed up by J. Sacks (ed.), *Orthodoxy Confronts Modernity* (Hoboken, NJ: Ktav, 1991), 13.
[5] S. Ahmed, *What Is Islam? The Importance of Being Islamic* (Princeton: Princeton University Press, 2016).

opinions on matters of truth. The one is rooted in conviction and experience; the other in aporia and a cold official detachment. What common ground could be identified between these two pluralisms?

One beginning point must lie with the assessment of the extent of Islamic ethic-legal versatility. Just as it is merely banal to claim that the *sharī'a* permits plurality, for the texts and the historic record admit no contrary view, it is hardly less banal to observe that it is so disparate a legal culture, its actual or potential jurisprudential techniques so protean, that one could find most things, or at least their starting point, if one set out to look for them with enough determination. Under the suasive pressure to conform exercised by Western elites and by the spectacle of Western material success, modern reformist pluralisms, sometimes based on the conative aims of Islamic law (*maqāsid al-sharī'a*), or on the notion of necessity and emergency (*nawāzil*), or even on prioritising Meccan over Medinan episodes of the founder's mission, are extensively theorised although much less widely disseminated; they are readily accessible in the writings of, for instance, Tariq Ramadan and Khaled Abou el Fadl, and Jocelyne Cesari has ably mapped many of them in her book *The Awakening of Muslim Democracy*.[6] Whether 'Islam', however this contested thing might persuasively be articulated, can incorporate a pluralism is not a question, therefore, and should

---

[6] J. Cesari, *The Awakening of Muslim Democracy: Religion, Modernity, and the State* (Cambridge: Cambridge University Press, 2014).

not detain us. For Muslims, wishing to establish pluralistic forms of life which might appeal not only to subaltern elites categorically detached from the world-view of their pre-modern elite predecessors, but to the grass roots, the more substantive question, instead, is likely to hinge on the answers to three related queries.

Firstly, has a positive hermeneutics of difference and the diversity of centres of knowing truly been a natural rather than an exceptional consequence of scriptural teaching? Secondly, if a Muslim pluralism of this kind exists as a faithful normativity, does it include forms which can be included in the 'overlapping consensus' required by modern liberal theories of national and international order, or is its logic too irreducible in its strangeness? Thirdly, what are the prospects for this clash of pluralisms, liberal and Muslim, in the current environment of retreat from liberal models across the Western world?

So our preliminary account of modernity's struggle against Cairo's dichotomised social topography and its decaying polycentrism will lead us in a plurality of directions; but these are necessary to enable a final hypothesis, which must bring to the surface a theological rather than a historical or sociological discourse, and will also be cautious and provisional, reflecting both the difficulty of defining Muslim normativities, and the current rapid flux in which Islamic and also Western habits of othering are being reshaped.

So, to the first of our questions. Cairo's old diversity can in part be seen as an entailment of Islam's techniques of localising the sacred, which allow a dispersal of authority and discourses. But what did pre-colonial Muslims mean by their toleration of unbelieving difference? Did this in practice simply ensue from sultanic incompetence, or from an attitude of indifferent contempt? The medieval handbooks on the status of tolerated minorities (*dhimma*), like so many other legal manuals of the time,[7] have to be understood as perfectionist tours de force rather than records of actual fact and practice. Where the strict rules were applied, which was not frequently, this was often a matter of pragmatism. Anver Emon, noting the great responsiveness of *dhimma* laws to context, identifies them not so much as theologically driven statutory instructions but as empirical constructs designed to protect the rule of law in polities in which, as today, elites are always hegemonic.[8] More instructive than the jurists' abstract theories and their inconsistent application is the archivally documented praxis of *qāḍī* courts and the administration of the Ottoman millet system, and this latter arrangement has been investigated by Karen Barkey in her study of Ottoman diversity management entitled *Empire of Difference*. "The centuries of Pax Ottomanica were relatively

---

[7] A very similar instance in which theory was able to depart from idealising and totalising visions to accommodate diversity, local exigencies and change is the question of gendered sacred spaces; see M.H. Katz, *Women in the Mosque: A History of Legal Thought and Social Practice* (New York: Columbia University Press, 2014).

[8] A.M. Emon, *Religious Pluralism and Islamic Law: 'Dhimmīs' and Others in the Empire of Law* (Oxford: Oxford University Press, 2012).

calm and free of ethnic or religious strife",⁹ she notes in framing her account of the markedly diverse Ottoman domains, with the main intolerance coming from Christians directed against Jews, who understandably preferred to live in Muslim neighbourhoods.¹⁰ Regional differences were also deeply and permanently enshrined in law.¹¹ The empire comprised a huge palimpsest over which different communities wrote their own scripts; it included far-flung networks of Hanafī and Shāfi'ī legists, Bektashi dervishes, gypsies, guild fraternities, Naqshbandīs and the Muslim others; but also stable unbelieving ecologies, of which the Orthodox, Armenian and Jewish were formally constituted as segments of the polity through the imperial grant of appointments to communal leaders. Patriarchs were rural landlords and tax farmers, and their powers over their flocks were far greater than those envisaged for religious communities in modern liberal democracies: they determined laws and administered justice insofar as this applied to litigation between co-religionists, and they collected taxes on behalf of the sultan. Minorities, as in Cairo, inhabited their own autonomous kinship networks and urban neighbourhoods, and other spaces as well, including distinct denominational sectors of the craft guilds. In this world, religionists could imagine the Ottoman

---

⁹ K. Barkey, *Empire of Difference: The Ottomans in Comparative Perspective* (New York: Cambridge University Press, 2008), 146.
¹⁰ Ibid., 149.
¹¹ C. Imber, *Ebu's-su'ud: The Islamic Legal Tradition* (Edinburgh: Edinburgh University Press, 1997), 44.

domain as a Jewish landscape, or Christian, or Islamic; all could claim to be coherent and stable perceptions, although the remote but finally controlling hand of the ruler, entitled *'ālem-penāh*, Refuge of the World, was always Islamic, which seemed constitutionally sensible; after all, only Muslims revered the founders of all the empire's official religions.

This stable diversity management paradigm certainly did not comprise the only potential reading of the Islamic juridical library; and yet since it endured for many centuries under the aegis of a polity that came to assume caliphal claims, it has a fair claim to be considered normatively Muslim. It is regularly cited as proof of Islam's recurrent desire for a world of stable difference, for instance by modern Balkan Muslim historians who feel threatened by Christian violence, or Palestinians who fear the same from Jews, and has occasionally inspired Europeans, eternally anxious about their own continent, which under Christian and then secular scientific auspices seemed to struggle with plurality more than did its Ottoman rival. As Noel Malcolm has shown, seventeenth-century Europeans polemicising about the reasons for their religious civil wars frequently inculcated a guilty introspection by describing the apparently successful Ottoman alternative.[12] In the age of Enlightenment, Johann Wolfgang von Goethe and Jean-Jacques Rousseau experimented with a very similar trope.

---

[12] N. Malcolm, *Useful Enemies: Islam and the Ottoman Empire in Western Political Thought, 1450–1750* (Oxford: Oxford University Press, 2019).

In Search of a Contemporary Sharī'a Discourse of Pluralism

In the aftermath of the Second World War, Arnold Toynbee, documenting the specifically European, Darwinian and Enlightenment etiology of the then recent mayhem, wrote that "the Islamic tradition [...] would seem to be a better ideal for meeting the social need of the times than the Western tradition", and here the author of *A Study of History* had the millet system significantly in mind.[13]

However, the currently regnant nation-state paradigm and the usual Habermasian strictures on the institutionalising of modular difference are unlikely to tolerate minorities writing as thickly as they did upon the Ottoman palimpsest. Liberal democracy, for the reasons cited by Benhabib, cannot devolve so much authority to minority groups: the modern state monopolises law-making, offering only a few grudging and nowadays hugely contested concessions to halakhic and *sharī'a* tribunals, or, in North America, to residual Native American codes. Under the sultans, Christian women's dress was typically regulated by Christian systems; in the modern European state, Muslim women's dress is increasingly a matter for government decision-making. We shall have more to say about this paradox of liberal democracy later in this lecture. But the most essential disjuncture between Ottoman and contemporary arrangements for subsidiary governance is that the Ottomans presupposed the indefinite perpetuity of overwritten scripts derived from

---

[13] A. Toynbee, *The World and the West: The B.B.C. Reith Lectures, 1952* (London: Oxford University Press, 1953), 30.

alternate revelations and sources of holiness which had been variously although not uncritically acknowledged in the Qur'an. Presumptively, the minorities were allowed to be abidingly different because the ethics and codes of the People of the Book were obscurely derived from God's revelation, albeit in earlier and abrogated redactions. Christians and Jews could be permitted to drink wine because God had, in past prophetic ages, not seen fit to prohibit it; and the jurists evolved a *fiqh* category of *sharā'i' man qablanā*, "the revealed codes of those who came before us", which could sometimes bind Islamic believers as well.[14] Because Islam's own laws were constantly debated and never generated an accepted canon of statutes prior to the modern period, it seemed natural to tolerate or even to assume this radical judicial polyvocality. Even God's real law, deduced as the *fiqh*, was understood to represent a work in progress. In other words, the Ottoman agglomeration of rules and congregations grew from a foundational rather than a pragmatic pluralism, so that minorities did not just cherish inherited folkways but insisted that they were privileged harbingers of a metaphysical truth which coordinated and gave meaning to their distinctive form of life. Enlightenment ideas of subjecting all laws and social practices to some overarching Kantian yardstick were absent: each script written over the well-protected domains was a complete discursive universe, entire of itself, even

---

[14] M.H. Kamali, *Principles of Islamic Jurisprudence* (Cambridge: Islamic Texts Society, 1991), 229–234.

though communities were vertically linked to the Sublime Porte by various security and fiscal mechanisms, and the sultan might occasionally read "mirrors for princes" which offered general notions about justice. The modules were far from equal in law, since *dhimma* rules imposed sumptuary, testimonial and other significant disabilities on non-Muslims; but, as though in compensation, these modules enjoyed a far greater degree of autonomy, presumption of unique rightness, and assurance about the identity of their descendants than is feasible in the centralised nation-states of the contemporary monoculture.

This, to transpose the argument now into a theological key, seems to comprise a recurrent and defining aspect of the charism of Ishmael. Emmanuel Levinas famously distinguishes Athens from Jerusalem by identifying Odysseus as the European wanderer who returns to his home, and hence to resolution and philosophical closure; while Abraham, as proto-Jewish wanderer, migrates into alterity; Talmudic discursiveness is therefore said to reject closure and embrace indeterminacy; Orthodox legal culture is pluralistic.[15] In the case of Ishmael we would add that if Jerusalem is the sign of a people – or, for Christians, of the Messiah who decisively discloses a singular truth, and is closure incarnate – then the Meccan sanctuary is the alterity into which Ishmael was exiled, but whose Black Stone signifies the Primordial Covenant itself; it is the place of congregation of souls before nations and religions were

---

[15] C. Davis, *Levinas: An Introduction* (Cambridge: Polity, 1996), 94.

instantiated. The Ishmaelite's migration, then, seems to be simultaneously to 'same' and 'other'. He is Odysseus but also Abraham: his legal codes will seek conclusions, unlike the beloved Talmud of Levinas, even though these are almost all conditional and open to contest; and this neatly encapsulates the typical pre-modern climate of Islamic legal and moral argument which was described recently by Thomas Bauer as the "culture of ambiguity".[16] Islam as a prophetic religion is passionate for truth, but historically is at ease with a panoply of methods, schools and formulations; and this was not experienced as a paradox.

Jurists vindicated this by welcoming the diverse opinions of the prophet's companions as an assurance of valid subsequent difference; the Egyptian author al-Suyūtī began his *The Generous Gifts of the Diversity of Ethico-legal Schools* with a *hadīth* which has the prophet say: "It would not please me were my Companions not to differ, for if they did not differ, there would be no mercy". Suyūtī remarks, savouring the sophisticated fallibilism (but not scepticism) of his jurisprudential culture:

> The diversity of ethico-legal schools [*madhāhib*] in religion is a tremendous blessing and grace, based in a subtle mystery which real scholars understand. I heard an ignorant man declare: "The Holy Prophet brought one law, so what is the reason for these four schools?" Bizarre, also, is

---

[16] T. Bauer, *Die Kultur der Ambiguität: eine andere Geschichte des Islams* (Berlin: Verlag der Weltreligionen, 2011).

the view of those who hurtfully try to show the superiority of some schools over others [...] in a way which recalls the tribalism and party-spirit of the Days of Ignorance ['asabiyya wa-hamiyyat al-jāhiliyya].17

Thus the forms of life supported by Ishmaelite scripture are indicatively diverse and valuably contested, even though the discursive tradition that is Islam is, in its regularly discovered consensual convergences, unmistakeably Islamic, a paradox that we still struggle to resolve.

So Muslim juridical debates on the Muslim and non-Muslim 'other' are not liable to ecclesiastical closure – for there is no magisterial centre – nor to the kind of rabbinical assurance that holds that without either temple or Messiah all is indeterminate and provisional. Certain *sharī'a* truths are *muhkam*, or *qat'ī*, decisive and unambiguous; and yet these occupy only a small fraction of the manuals of law, which are not embarrassed to describe verdicts as *zannī*, or conjectural. It was this culture of ambiguity which enabled the thick pluralism of Ottoman Cairo;18 by contrast, the pluralism of modern liberal states appears decidedly thin, being based not in ontology but in prudential and pragmatic techniques for social management rooted in the insistence that the state be innocent of any metaphysical

---

17 Jalāl al-Dīn al-Suyūtī, *Jazīl al-mawāhib fi'khtilāf al-madhāhib*, ed. 'Abd al-Qayyūm al-Bastāwī (Cairo: Dār al-I'tisām, 1989), 20.
18 Despite the claims of nationalist historians, Egypt was a very characteristic Ottoman province; see E. Toledano, *State and Society in Mid-Nineteenth-Century Egypt* (Cambridge: Cambridge University Press, 1990).

claims. As the French government has found in its inheritance of the *Code Napoléon*, an ethico-legal national system based on reason and science will tend to seek singular outcomes, since reason, unlike the annoyingly polysemic oracles of revelation, insists that only one truth can be correct. This is why the state, buoyed by a triumphalist rationalism, knows how Muslim women should dress better than the women themselves.[19]

Ishmael's Great Sanctuary in Mecca is also the site at which God's text of difficult polysemy is disclosed. Qur'ān means not reason but recital; logos, more or less in the ancient sense; as *kalām Allāh al-qadīm* it is held to be uncreated; and so Ishmael's city is the point where space-time itself is interrupted and the unseen audibly appears. It is this logos which emerges as the point of light in every *mihrāb*, in every little Cairene mosque, reconnecting tired humans with ontology. As light it is universal and formless; its *baraka* is everywhere: the meta-text exists without race or gender;[20] and its first temple is in the symbolic hearth of humanity, the Mother of Cities. So Ishmael, interred in the sanctuary, presents the summative and universal evolutions of Abraham's purpose: the blood of Egypt, the Bible's favourite symbol of an unclean alterity, is mingled with his own; so that the Ishmaelite, Hagarene

---

[19] J. Baubérot, *La laïcité falsifiée* (Paris: La Découverte, 2012), 85–102.
[20] *Qur'ān* is grammatically masculine, but revelation is also *umm al-kitāb*, Mother of the Book (3:7); revealed in *umm al-qurā*, the Mother of Cities (6:92).

In Search of a Contemporary Shariʿa Discourse of Pluralism

prophet can one day declare, in the sanctuary: "I am sent to all mankind".[21]

So the millet system, the protean but God-fearing flux of *shariʿa* discourse, and the many-centred maze of Islamic urban forms can be seen as the interrelated outcomes of a founding narrative which purposively includes alterity and difference. The logos, when its Arabic is read, is hence a psalm to difference. Shining first in a town of paradigmatic Arabian particularity, the text embeds a sweeping and universal purport, beginning with praise to God, who is titled Lord of the Worlds. Fred Donner is so taken by the ecumenism of the Qur'an that he proposes that early Islam was a kind of inclusive monotheistic piety which for generations included Christians and Jews within its ranks.[22] Ethnic difference is of little interest to the scripture, while the Prophetic biography repeats the insistence that the fierce particularism of the Arab tribes must be overcome. Certainly the sources record that the founder's apostles conspicuously included Persians, Abyssinians and Byzantines, each of them a symbol of proleptic anticipation of Islam's triumphant expansion and inclusion.

The ontology of the scripture heard as logos may be experienced (Louis Massignon's famous observation) as prior in significance to its discursive content. But the logos, shining in the *miḥrābs* of Egypt and now also resonating

---

[21] Bukhārī, Tayammum, 1.
[22] F.M. Donner, *Muhammad and the Believers: At the Origins of Islam* (Cambridge, MA: Harvard University Press, 2012).

in the streets outside thanks to Radio Cairo, demonstrates the further enigma referred to by Patricia Crone with her observations about its non-referentiality. The scripture is readily detached from its real or legendary *Sitz im Leben*, it is a universalising commentary on the *historia monotheistica*, affirming the exemplum figures of the Bible, but also, in a way which has puzzled many, given its Western Arabian provincial cradle, vaulting over them with the annunciation of a universal providence which, as it says, has sent "a guide to every people" (13:7). The text exuberantly instructs us to contemplate the diversity of the natural world and of humanity: *ikhtilāfu alsinatikum wa-alwānikum*, the difference of your languages and colours, which are of God's signs (30:22). The logos 'sent down' in the most monocultural of Arabian places, to the very Arabian Man of Praise, is a threnody of difference which hails the world as a carnival of signifiers, and this includes humanity. "Had God willed He would have made you a single people, but [He wished] to test you in what He has given you; so vie with one another in good works" (5:48).

Holiness is everywhere, not just in Heaven. Hebrew biblical and midrashic tales are repristinated and reconfigured, but without the master-signifier of a particularist people; and "there is no people among whom a Warner has not passed" (35:24). The Babel legend which was constructed by the Yahwist authors as a sign that linguistic multiplicity is a punishment, has supplied a *locus classicus* for monoculturalist readings of the Bible since the time of Josephus; only recently have troubled Christians strained, against the evident plain sense of the text, to reposition it as an ironic affirmation of diversity.[23] Yet the story is absent from the Qur'an, which instead presents linguistic multiplicity as a grace; plural expression, not univocality, is God's way in creation; and it is a stable blessing, not a provisional compromise. Those who, like Crone again, like to see nascent Islam as an Arab nativism, have not noticed that the text does not mention the Arab people even once, although it decries their religion. It is distinctive in its xenophilia.

So old Cairo, which looked to Napoleon's scientists like a body with arteries but no heart, does indeed have a heart: the logos refulgent in the *mihrābs* and the little roadways which the scientists could not hear, but which the Cairene working classes absorb in every waking moment. Despite its radical outward confusion and unreason, the old city is unified by this logos, and the ideologies of progress in the past two centuries have failed to produce a successful rival. Ishmael, the half-gentile sign of Islam's inclusiveness, presides over a strong heterogeneity made possible ultimately by a vertical integration not to the state, but to the Muslim God, thanks to the belief in the sacrality of the local and in the omnipresence of the logos.

To turn back, then, to our quest as anxious moderns, which as we have seen cannot be for an Islamic pluralism, as this has been natively Islamic since the time of the Book and the Companions, but rather for a space permitting dialogue between an already empirically and scripturally

---

[23] E.g. T. Hiebert, "The Tower of Babel and the Origin of the World's Cultures", *Journal of Biblical Literature* 126 (2007) 29–58.

existent Ishmaelite logic of diversity with the pluralisms which are taken, at least in theory, to be an important constituent of liberal political culture; to return to our geographical trope: can the no man's land between old and new Cairo be a dwelling place not only for courtesans and fundamentalists, but for stable and moral hybrids whose discourse makes sense to both sides?

Unfortunately, any such dialogue, or any claimed cohabitation of a space of overlapping consensus, has been complexified by the major erosion of Islamic pluralisms by modernity. Localised expressions of charisma are fought by secularist regimes and also by Salafists, and are withering. On the political level we have already observed how the onset of modern nation-state narratives and techniques served to diminish or terminate minority existence in Cairo; and the same can be observed in the writing of Orhan Pamuk as he walks through Istanbul's former Greek quarters;[24] a very comparable mood of *huzn*, melancholia, is evoked by an ex-Jewish *mellah* in Morocco, or districts of Lahore historically shaped by a Sikh presence; the loss of minorities is a very general aspect of the modern Muslim condition and may well be exacerbating its dysfunction. Mark Mazower calls his history of Salonica *City of Ghosts*: the Sephardic majority inhabitants of the Thracian city, prospering tranquilly under the Pax Ottomana, were incorporated into the modern Greek state in 1912; within three decades they perished at Auschwitz, and the plural structure of their city is

---

[24] O. Pamuk, *Istanbul: Memories of a City* (London: Faber & Faber, 2006).

In Search of a Contemporary Sharī'a Discourse of Pluralism

now deeply forgotten.[25] The Westphalian polity assumes a paradigm of national belonging and what John Rawls calls a presumption of consensus, and, as Europe's twentieth century demonstrated, boasts a very uneven record, often tending to work towards the dilution, assimilation or removal of modules of significant difference.

In very recent times the Muslim nation-state has further tightened the permitted paradigms of belonging by securitising and homogenising the centre's relationship with Islam. Atatürk was the precursor, with his paradoxically simultaneous creation of a secular polity and a nationalised religious hierarchy. Elsewhere, in most Arab countries now, particularly since 11 September 2001, the hegemonic elites have worked to create a unified, compliant Islamic normativity and an apparatus of state seminaries whose graduates read out centrally issued sermons preaching obedience to the state and avoiding the discussion of sensitive issues such as poverty and official corruption. Independent homilies are impossible, and the ancient tradition of circles of instruction in mosques or madrasas in which scriptural interpretation could be pursued entirely free of sultanic supervision has become perilous or non-existent. Once again, modernisation, for all its claims, has in practice proved very allergic to heteronomy.

This modernised, homogenised, depluralised Islam, now often reconfigured by state actors against an insurrectionist

---

[25] M. Mazower, *Salonica, City of Ghosts: Christians, Muslims and Jews, 1430–1950* (London: Harper, 2005).

Salafism which is itself inimical to diversity, is today asked to theorise and deliver a modern discourse of a Muslim pluralism. In what way is this a feasible demand?

Some distinguished writing is already going on in response to what is clearly one of the momentous global questions of our day. I have mentioned Anver Emon's close discussion of Islamicate historical practice towards minorities, and he has also written on Muslim equivalents of natural law theory and the tradition's capacity to engage with systems which purport to be grounded in reason alone.[26] There is also Andrew March's ambitious monograph *Islam and Liberal Citizenship*: March confesses his outsider status but concludes that such a consensus can be found.[27] Also of intellectual interest is the volume by Christian Joppke and John Torpey, *Legal Integration of Islam*.[28] Mohammad Fadel has likewise contributed significantly to the discussion.[29] All conclude affirmatively: that *sharī'a* discourse, or some recognisable configuration of it, is amenable to self-inclusion in Rawls' overlapping consensus. These works mainly deal with Islamic ethical

---

[26] A.M. Emon/M. Levering/D. Novak, *Natural Law: A Jewish, Christian, and Islamic Trialogue* (Oxford: Oxford University Press, 2014).

[27] A.F. March, *Islam and Liberal Citizenship: The Search for an Overlapping Consensus* (New York: Oxford University Press, 2009).

[28] C. Joppke/J. Torpey, *Legal Integration of Islam: A Transatlantic Comparison* (Cambridge, MA: Harvard University Press, 2013).

[29] M. Fadel, "The True, the Good and the Reasonable: The Theological and Ethical Roots of Public Reason in Islamic Law", *Canadian Journal of Law & Jurisprudence* 21 (2008) 5–69.

and paralegal integration in Western democracies, and do not acknowledge the increasing fixity of state-securitised Muslim discourse in majority Muslim countries. However, it is worth noting that Muslim diasporic communities continue to be significantly networked in various ways with the hierarchies of those countries: witness the iconic and widely publicised ejection in 2017 of the Salafist imam from the Saudi-sponsored central mosque of Brussels, whose influence was believed to have radicalised a number of the capital's Arab youth.[30] Such challenges to allied regimes are, however, unusual, and one is perhaps permitted to note the ironic situation of liberal European governments as they engage closely with religious officials and advisors appointed by authoritarian regimes, in the attempt to create a more local 'European' Islam which it is hoped will be amenable to liberalisation. France is currently working with monarchical and dirigiste Morocco to develop consistent imam training programmes suitable for the secular republic.[31] Other ironies are not far to seek.

---

[30] M. Birnbaum/Q. Ariès, "Belgium Ends Saudi Mosque Lease, Citing 'Foreign Interference' and Extremism", *The Washington Post*, 19 March 2018, available at https://www.washingtonpost.com/world/europe/belgium-ends-saudi-mosque-lease-citing-foreign-interference-and-extremism/2018/03/19/eebd3912-2b7a-11e8-8dc9-3b51e028b845_story.html (accessed 5 December 2019).

[31] A.M. Wainscott, "Defending Islamic Education: War on Terror Discourse and Religious Education in Twenty-First-Century Morocco", *The Journal of North African Studies* 20 (2015) 635–653.

We have several times referred to the Rawlsian doctrine of the overlapping consensus, and it seems appropriate now to probe further into the claims made in the above works for the *sharī'a*'s capacity to partake in this. The consensus in question is a concept which largely replaces older and more ambitious Enlightenment convictions about the objective discernibility of public reason, with a late-twentieth-century aversion to the preferences of 'good people', a category which Rawls leaves fairly indeterminate but which presumptively denotes the post-Enlightenment reasonable elite of Anglo-America. Religion, perhaps notably non-Western religion, understandably chafes under this authority, and across the Muslim world and elsewhere Islamists in particular see in this presumption of elite Occidental normativity an imperial hegemonic othering and objectification of themselves. Religions, defined as comprehensive doctrines, are expected, in the Western-dominated globalised order, to reinvent themselves in terms acceptable to the 'good people', to join the alleged global consensus on rights and liberties. In the name of a pluralistic culture, non-Western pluralisms and pluralities are to be abolished or entirely re-signified.

Islamic cultures are naturally not alone in producing dissidents against this undemocratic and prescriptive view of national and international citizenship. Despite a common trope which holds that Islam, possessed of its own public law in the form of the *sharī'a*, is distinctively or uniquely troubling to the Enlightenment vision of a faith-neutral public space which relegates religion to a sphere of irrelevant private choices, most and perhaps all religions insist that their moral vision has implications for believers' proper action in the public square, and that the liberal world must therefore try to tolerate real ethical difference. Hence of the 53 sovereign legislatures of the Commonwealth, 35 deem homosexual practice a criminal act, typically because of the culture of religiously active populations; Secretary-General Baroness Patricia Scotland, whose inculturation took place in North London, critiques the absence of a public reason in those countries akin to her own. Again the question is: whose justice, which rationality? Alasdair MacIntyre, while averse to relativism, reminds us that rationality cannot be neutral but is always shaped by tradition. Baroness Scotland's public reasons are shaped by her environment; the public reasons of Ghanaian bishops are taken to be no less reasonable, but are rooted in a different conceptual scheme. To break this kind of impasse MacIntyre offers a sort of evolutionary hope that the encounter of rival social beliefs will produce an epistemic crisis in some, yielding a convergence in the longer term. Dissidents will finally be out-narrated, and non-Western outliers may be tolerated as symptomatic of nothing more worrying than a time deficit.

Among Muslims, equipped already with a different pluralistic tradition, this epistemic crisis has been well-advanced since Bonaparte's era; accounting for the compliant modernism voiced by the inhabitants of the gated communities on the Muqattam, and the anti-traditionalism of the elite theorists who compose the Arab Human Development Reports which, as Joseph Massad has shown, consistently exclude indigenous Arab definitions of human fulfilment.³² Public reasons, as articulated internationally, are those of a Western or Westernised elite consensus, and signally decline to consult cultural alterities. The Universal Declaration of Human Rights was first drafted by Charles Malik, the generally anti-Muslim founder of the Lebanese Front; for this Catholic and Europhile revanchist, Islam, having fallen at the hurdle of Muʻtazilism, could neither produce real universals, nor recognise them, in stark contrast to the deep traditions of Western thought.³³

Malik follows a line of cultured despisers stretching back to Joseph-Ernest Renan and forward to Joseph Ratzinger in our own times, which imagines that Muslim theology with its unshakeably high view of revelation and its Ashʻarite 'command ethics' is the primal paradigm of the anti-rationalist 'other' of Latin Christendom and the *lumières* which supplanted it. Of all religious traditions it is the darkest of such Others, and should be the most vigorously excluded from the public conversation; hence, probably, Newt Gingrich's strangely fearful description of

---

³² J.A. Massad, *Islam in Liberalism* (Chicago: University of Chicago Press, 2015), 177-180, 194-195. Cf. R. Guénon, *The Crisis of the Modern World* (London: Luzac & Co., 1962), 97: "In the West people are apt to imagine that these vociferous but not very numerous individuals represent the actual Orient, whereas actually their influence is really not as widespread nor as deep as it may appear: this false impression is easily accounted for by the fact that the West is unacquainted with the true Orientals, who moreover do not go out of their way to make themselves known, while it is only the modernists, if one may so style them, who draw attention to themselves, talk, write, and engage in all manner of agitation".

³³ Cf. E.W. Said, *Out of Place: A Memoir* (London: Granta, 1999), 263-269.

sharīʿa as a "mortal threat" to America,[34] and the legal proscription of something called Sharia law in a number of US states. It is feared as an unstable corrosive substance which somehow will destroy the essential workings of the constitution. Yet recent work on Ashʿarism and Islamic law shows that Islam does of course recognise the validity of public reason arguments; Emon and Fadel have amply demonstrated this. Josef van Ess even writes this: "Christianity speaks of the 'mysteries' of faith; Islam has nothing like that. For Saint Paul, reason belongs to the realm of the 'flesh', for Muslims, reason, *ʿaql*, has always been the chief faculty granted human beings by God".[35] Islamic art, too, bodies forth the Muslim soul's sense of reasoned and objective geometry: "In the mosque the God of mathematics seems at work, whereas the cathedral looks more like a kind of Grand Guignol of martyred saints".[36] The presumption of a wild Oriental fideistic irrationality, dominant in Bonaparte's time, is fading steadily.

Mohammad Fadel, drawing on an abundance of scriptural and medieval texts, concludes that

> Islamic jurisprudence grew to recognize the legitimacy of rule-making based on arguments whose premises

---

[34] Massad, *Islam in Liberalism*, 58.
[35] J. van Ess, *The Flowering of Muslim Theology* (Cambridge, MA: Harvard University Press, 2006), 153–154.
[36] H. Ree, *The Human Comedy of Chess: A Grandmaster's Chronicles* (Milford, CT: Russell Enterprises, 1999), 143, referring to the *mezquita* of Córdoba.

> – while consistent with revelation – were non-revelatory and therefore that Islamic law, as a historical matter, recognized the legitimacy of public reason arguments [...].[37]

In the later centuries of Islam, Māturīdī tradition in particular, according to Sabine Schmidtke, still somewhat marginalised by Oriental studies, was well-known for its rationalising epistemology; Islam begins with a revelation which deploys reasoned arguments (*nazar, ilzām*), and grows through time to reach a very acute emphasis on the principle of reason and, as Emon understands it, natural law. And whereas the rights considered innate by liberal theory prove hard for recent secular philosophy to define, appearing as attempts to conjure universals and intrinsic value from the dumb dead matter of the world, the Māturīdī tradition affirms rights as innate in all human beings whatever their later religious trajectory; this is the principle of *'ismat al-ādamiyya*, the inherent inviolability of all of Adamic descent, which has been studied by Recep Şentürk.[38] Muslim theology turns out to generate moral universals and the presumption of human worth and rights much more readily, or thickly, than secular materialism.

Armed with this twin-pointed sword, Muslims evidently can join modernity's public conversation. Their

---

[37] Fadel, "The True, the Good and the Reasonable", 5.
[38] R. Şentürk, "Sociology of Rights: 'I Am Therefore I Have Rights': Human Rights in Islam between Universalistic and Communalistic Perspectives", *Muslim World Journal of Human Rights* 2/1 (2005) 1–31, on p. 5.

comprehensive doctrines, looked on with suspicion by many secular critics, turn out to yield very thick public reasons when compared with atheistic belief systems. Richard Rorty dismisses Kantian grounds for altruism in favour of a Whiggish sort of historical progressism: what is better is what we feel we have conscientiously progressed towards. Again, the resultant values will persuade only inhabitants of his own silo. But reasoned theism seems to furnish better grounds, and if its arguments interrogate some of the social beliefs to which Rorty's fellow silo-dwellers have migrated, then it has offered the prospect of widening and invigorating the overlapping consensus. It has not stepped outside it, although it is not ignorant of an outside.

Let us briefly give examples of how this might look. Arguments sourced in religious conceptual schemes will contribute meaningfully to the space's public reason to different degrees. Inaccessible arguments might include, for instance, a Muslim public claim that the French republic ought to reduce and ultimately eliminate the eating of pork. The scriptural prohibition might perhaps have an *'illa*, a determinative rational cause, but it has not convincingly been found yet.

More accessible would be an argument by, say, Muslim parliamentarians, that alcohol consumption should be restricted. This, too, is based on a scriptural ban; but the *'illa* is intelligible and not religion-specific. The American Medical Association reports that in 92% of cases perpetrators of domestic violence were using alcohol at the time of the offence.³⁹ A recent study in *The Lancet* shows the negative health outcomes of even moderate alcohol intake.⁴⁰ On grounds of women's rights and public health, then, it appears that Muslims could easily launch a challenge to historically originated customs of legal alcohol manufacture, trafficking and consumption in Western democracies and globally. Western resistance to this challenge is likely to be significantly less rational than the *sharīʿa* reasons being advanced.

These are two simple instances of how a *sharīʿa* discourse might with different degrees of success enter public debates and controversies, and contribute to what Rawls calls "fair social cooperation". So many others could be imagined that one is tempted to consider secularist presumptions of religious irrationalism and soteriocentricity as prejudicial. *Sharīʿa*, particularly in its Hanafī and Māturīdī expression which proposes that *al-aṣl al-taʿlīl*, that there is a presumption that God's laws are rational and have public reason explications, turns out to be eminently, though not in every case, suited to participation in liberal democratic discussions, despite the presuppositions of Ratzinger and Gingrich.

We need to press further here. Emon, March and Fadel confirm this sense that Islam's polycentric tradition can

---

³⁹ Cf. https://www.verywellmind.com/domestic-abuse-and-alcohol-62643 (accessed 5 December 2019).

⁴⁰ M.G. Griswold *et al.*, "Alcohol Use and Burden for 195 Countries and Territories, 1990–2016: A Systematic Analysis for the Global Burden of Disease Study 2016", *The Lancet* 392 (2018) 1015–1035.

host burdens of proof sufficient to access our liberal public square. However, their works predate the most recent shift in Occidental discourse. We have already noted the shrinking of Islamic plurivocality ensuing from modernisation, fundamentalism, and the governmentalising of Islam in the Muslim world. This has often been accompanied by a retreat into a fideism which will certainly obstruct any persuasive Muslim entrance into the public square. Conversely, we should observe that the Western liberal universe has also recently entered a condition of flux, as the "fatalism of progress" assumed by Rawls and Rorty is challenged by new forms of national populism, which to many seem highly regressive. Muslims instructed to be pluralistic bring their offerings to a table which they increasingly experience as non-rational and also non-secular. In his major address of 10 January 2019 to students at the American University in Cairo, an academy for children of Egypt's Anglophone governance elite, Mike Pompeo explained how his evangelical religious beliefs shape his policy in the Middle East. He always keeps a Bible on his desk, and he knows that his God wants him to punish Iran and stand by Israel.[41]

The intense religionising of the discourse of the West's exemplary Enlightenment republic is widely noted in the

---

[41] R. Wright, "Pompeo and His Bible Define U.S. Policy in the Middle East", *The New Yorker*, 10 January 2019, available at https://www.newyorker.com/news/our-columnists/pompeo-and-his-bible-define-us-policy-in-the-middle-east (accessed 5 December 2019).

Muslim world, whose commentators are struggling to interpret the current Christianisation of a great Satan which confusingly still urges religion-state separation in Muslim countries. It directly challenges the dichotomising assumption of Occidental reasonableness which the East has confronted since Napoleon's incursion. However, this, and its attendant chauvinisms, should not logically compel a Muslim retreat from the principle of a global conversation of public reasons, however unreasonable and one-sided the Occident's public reasons might often seem to be.

In Europe, where Muslims are also asked to exchange their own pluralism for one of Western making, there is a cognate and no less rapid transformation afoot. The growing visibility of Muslim minorities, and a recent increase in the number of refugees and asylum seekers, has been a major factor in the rise of national populism across the continent. The French rationalist legacy still struggles with Muslim difference, banning long skirts in schools, 'burkinis', and face veils, while Marine Le Pen explicitly deploys feminism as a weapon against the Muslim presence in France.[42] In England, Muslims hoping to join the 'rational' public square are reminded that 31% of Brexit Leave voters accept the Great Replacement theory, which holds that elites are plotting to replace the indigenous working classes with low-salary Muslim immigrants.[43] A

---

[42] Baubérot, *La laïcité falsifiée*, 93.
[43] N. Nougayrède, "Europe Is in the Grip of Conspiracy Theories – Will They Define Its Elections?", *The Guardian*, 1 February 2019, available at

recent Chatham House survey shows that most British people want to see an end to all Muslim immigration;[44] in Germany 60% of the population claim that Islam does not belong in their country, a view conspicuously supported by the minister of the interior.[45] The 2018 study by Roger Eatwell and Matthew Goodwin on national populism points to a new style of politics across Europe: Islamophobic, pro-Israel, pro-gay, and Eurosceptic, which cannot be simply classified as right-wing. Muslimness is the unifying theme for these movements and is specifically targeted: Norway's minister of immigration tells Muslims: "Here we eat pork, drink alcohol, and show our faces. You must abide by the values, laws and regulations that are in Norway when you come here".[46] In Italy, Matteo Salvini criticises an Italian-Egyptian singer's winning the Sanremo Italian song competition.[47] Across the continent, *hijāb* and

https://www.theguardian.com/commentisfree/2019/feb/01/europe-conspiracy-theories-eu-elections (accessed 5 December 2019).

[44] R. Eatwell/M. Goodwin, *National Populism: The Revolt Against Liberal Democracy* (London: Pelican, 2018), 111.

[45] Ibid., 277.

[46] P. Walker, "Norway Integration Minister Faces Resignation Calls after Telling Muslims 'We Eat Pork and Drink Alcohol'", *The Independent*, 21 October 2016, available at https://www.independent.co.uk/news/world/europe/norway-integration-minister-muslim-eat-pork-drink-alcohol-show-face-sylvi-listhaug-a7372991.html (accessed 5 December 2019).

[47] A. Giuffrida, "Italian-Egyptian Singer's Victory Angers Matteo Salvini", *The Guardian*, 11 February 2019, available at https://www.theguardian.com/world/2019/feb/11/italian-egyptian-mahmood-singers-victory-angers-matteo-salvini (accessed 5 December 2019).

niqāb bans smack minorities into remembering their own deplorability. So we might say that today's secular reason has reasons that reason knows nothing of. The public square has simply not become what Rawls, Jürgen Habermas and Francis Fukuyama expected in predicting the steady onward march of tolerant rationality. And as Eatwell and Goodwin observe, populism is growing and will not vanish readily.

Surrounded by such cultured despisers on the continent, which is almost a synonym for liberal democracy but in which liberalism is becoming coercive and the overlapping consensus has shifted markedly, Muslims are nonetheless instructed by elites not to retreat into isolation but to iterate a pluralism of an intelligibly Western kind. However, to the confusion of governments, they are not a single pair of ears. Muslims in Europe are displaying something of the polycentric pattern of old Cairo: metropolitan Islam in Europe is startlingly heteronomic; the bazaars of Birmingham and Hamburg present a polyglot carnival; the cadences of the Qur'an hang in the air as though to validate this. Yet the deep defining charism of Ishmael has not been disguised, and here, in defence of the old Cairene *hāra*-dwellers with their patience and their humour, we would propose a return to the Ishmael and Hagar trope, denoting the poor, the refugee and asylum seeker, the ethnically problematic, the single mother, recalling that the Muslim God announces: "I am with the broken-hearted".[48]

---

[48] Abū Nuʿaym al-Isfahānī, *Hilyat al-awliyāʾ wa-tabaqāt al-asfiyāʾ* (Cairo: al-Khanjī, 1351–1357AH), II, 364.

The voiceless urban poor of Cairo, concurrently disdained by Western monoculturalists and by Muslim fundamentalists, are likely, from this liberative scriptural optic, to be a privileged site of divine pleasure and support.

As coercive liberal elites demand compliance with their social beliefs in the name of pluralism,[49] Muslim theology increasingly stresses this withness. Islamic kerygma, like many biblical versions, announces a God who favours not governance elites, neo-liberal and usurious capital concentration, or the tribal 'ignorance', *jāhiliyya*, of national populism, but the victims of all of these things. These victims stubbornly refuse a pluralism which in reality demands nothing other than compliance; and so they are now challenged to present, as Ishmaelite paradigms of faithful outsiderness, a theology of the Great Sanctuary which allows intersubjectivity and heteronomy to thrive in an age of reducing cultures, species, forms of life, and the other *vestigia Dei* which scripture commands us to celebrate and not to iron out under modernity's univocal but difficult ratio.

---

[49] Note the view of the former president of the American University of Beirut, John Waterbury: "I believe that basic tendencies in regional culture and in religious practice must be overcome rather than utilized in any efforts to promote pluralism and democracy", cited in Massad, *Islam in Liberalism*, 54.

Notes on Contributors

Jocelyne Cesari holds the Chair of Religion and Politics at the University of Birmingham, is senior fellow at Georgetown University's Berkley Center for Religion, Peace & World Affairs, T.J. Dermot Dunphy Visiting Professor of Religion, Violence, and Peacebuilding at Harvard Divinity School, and was President of the European Academy of Religion (2018–2019). Her most recent books are: *What is Political Islam?* (Lynne Rienner Publishers, 2018), International Studies Association 2019 "Religion and International Relations Book Award" honorable mention; *Islam, Gender, and Democracy in Comparative Perspective* (Oxford University Press, 2017), co-authored with José Casanova.

Craig Calhoun is professor of Social Sciences at Arizona State University. He was previously Director of the London School of Economics, President of the Social Science Research Council, and a professor at both NYU, Columbia, and UNC at Chapel Hill. His books include *The Roots of Radicalism: Tradition, the Public Sphere, and Early Nineteenth-Century Social Movements* (University of Chicago Press, 2012), *Critical Social Theory: Culture, History, and the*

Challenge of Difference (Wiley, 1995), and *Does Capitalism Have a Future?* (Oxford University Press, 2013), co-edited with Immanuel Wallerstein, Randall Collins, Michael Mann and Georgi Derluguian.

Maureen Junker-Kenny is professor of Theology and fellow of Trinity College Dublin. Her publications include: *Religion and Public Reason: A Comparison of the Positions of John Rawls, Jürgen Habermas and Paul Ricoeur* (De Gruyter, 2014); *Approaches to Theological Ethics: Sources, Traditions, Visions* (T&T Clark, 2019); *Habermas on Religion* (*European Journal for Philosophy of Religion*, 2019 special issue). Her research interests are religion and public reason, Jürgen Habermas, Paul Ricoeur, Friedrich Schleiermacher and theology in modernity, biomedical ethics.

Sophie Nordmann teaches Jewish Thought and Philosophy at the École Pratique des Hautes Études in Paris. Her research focuses particularly on German Jewish philosophers (Hermann Cohen, Franz Rosenzweig, Gershom Scholem) in the nineteenth and twentieth centuries and on the relationship between Jewish thought and philosophy in French contemporary thought (École juive de Paris, André Neher, Emmanuel Levinas). Her most recent book is *Levinas et la philosophie judéo-allemande* (Vrin, 2017).

Tim Winter is university lecturer in Islamic Studies in the Faculty of Divinity, University of Cambridge, and Dean of the Cambridge Muslim College. His books include *The Cambridge Companion to Classical Islamic Theology* (Cambridge University Press, 2008), and, as Abdal Hakim Murad, *Bombing without Moonlight: The Origins of Suicidal Terrorism* (Amal Press, 2008) and *Commentary on the Eleventh Contentions* (The Quilliam Press, 2012).

Name Index

Abou el Fadl, Khaled 104
Abraham 97, 102, 111, 112, 114
Abu-Lughod, Lila 100
Ahmed, Shahab 103
Anderson, Benedict 38
Ariès, Quentin 121
Aristotle 62
Atatürk, Mustafa Kemal 119
Augustine of Hippo 12, 42

Barash, Jeffrey A. 79
Barkey, Karen 106, 107
Baubérot, Jean 114, 130
Bauer, Thomas 112
Beaumont, Justin 11
Benhabib, Seyla 99, 109
Bhargava, Rajeev 27
Birnbaum, Michael 121
Bleich, J. David 103
Böckenförde, Ernst-Wolfgang 63–65
Bourdieu, Pierre 51
Bourel, Dominique 80
Buber, Martin 41, 79–87, 92, 93

Cahill, Lisa S. 61
Calhoun, Craig 10, 19, 26, 27, 30, 38, 51, 54
Callixtus III, pope (Alfons de Borja) 102
Casanova, José 27
Cesari, Jocelyne 9, 104
Christerson, Brad 24
Cohen, Hermann 77–79, 92, 93

Coleman, James S. 51
Crone, Patricia 116, 117

Damasio, Antonio 48
Davis, Colin 111
Donner, Fred M. 115
Doudna, Jennifer A. 45
Dubnow, Simon 92
Durkheim, Émile 10
Düwell, Marcus 44

Eatwell, Roger 131, 132
Eckholt, Margit 72, 73
Emon, Anver M. 106, 120, 125, 126, 128
Engels, Friedrich 35
Ess, Josef van 125

Fadel, Mohammad 120, 125, 126, 128
Flory, Richard W. 24
Foucault, Michel 39, 40
Fukuyama, Francis 132

Gingrich, Newt 124, 128
Giuffrida, Angela 131
Goethe, J. Wolfgang von 108
Goodwin, Matthew 131, 132
Gorski, Philip S. 54
Griswold, Max G. 128
Guénon, René 124

Habermas, Jürgen 29, 53, 59, 60, 63–65, 68, 70–72, 132
Haferkamp, Hans 51
Hagar 132
Haker, Hille 61
Hanke, Lewis 44
Harari, Yuval N. 48

EuARe Lectures

Herzl, Theodor 14, 76
Hiebert, Theodore 117
Hirji, Zulfikar 102
Hobbes, Thomas 49, 50
Hollenbach, David 58
Hübenthal, Christoph 72
Hünermann, Peter 73
Hurlbut, J. Benjamin 45

Imber, Colin 107
Isaac, Jeffrey C. 35
al-Isfahānī, Abū Nuʻaym 132
Ishmael 97, 111, 114, 117, 132

Jasanoff, Sheila 46
Joppke, Christian 120
Juergensmeyer, Mark 26, 27
Juhant, Janez 73
Junker-Kenny, Maureen 10, 57, 61, 67

Kamali, Mohammad H. 110
Kant, Immanuel 41, 63, 67, 77
Kantorowicz, Ernst 43
Katz, Marion H. 106
Kobusch, Theo 62
Kropotkin, Peter 83

Le Pen, Marine 130
Lenin, Vladimir 83
Lenk, Hans 68
Lescourret, Marie-Anne 79
Levering, Matthew 120
Levinas, Emmanuel 41, 111, 112
Lovejoy, Arthur O. 43
Löwy, Michael 82, 83

MacIntyre, Alasdair 123
Malcolm, Noel 108

Malik, Charles 124
March, Andrew F. 120, 128
Marshall, Gordon 39
Marty, Martin E. 26
Marx, Karl 35, 83
Massad, Joseph A. 123–125, 133
Massignon, Louis 115
Masuzawa, Tomoko 25
Mazower, Mark 118, 119
Mendes-Flohr, Paul 79, 82
Mendieta, Eduardo 11
Messi Metogo, Eloi 61
Moses 86, 87
Mottahedeh, Roy P. 102
Muhammad 15

Nadel, Siegfried F. 38
Nagl-Docekal, Herta 58, 66–68
Napoleon I Bonaparte 95, 98, 101, 117, 123, 125, 130
Nasser, Gamal A. 97
Nordmann, Sophie 14, 75, 79
Nougayrède, Natalie 130
Novak, David 120

Odysseus 111, 112
O'Neill, Onora 60

Pamuk, Orhan 118
Parvin, Manoucher 15
Paul the Apostle 125
Pharo, Lars K. 44
Plato 42, 85
Podus, Deborah 25
Pompeo, Mike 129
Proudhon, Pierre-Joseph 83

Ramadan, Tariq 104
Ratzinger, Joseph 63, 124, 128

Name Index

Rawls, John 60, 63, 68, 69, 71, 89, 119, 120, 122, 128, 129, 132
Ree, Hans 125
Renan, Joseph-Ernest 124
Ricoeur, Paul 60, 63, 68, 71, 73
Roof, Wade C. 26
Rorty, Richard 127, 129
Rosa, Hartmut 35
Rousseau, Jean-Jacques 62, 108

Sacks, Jonathan 103
Said, Edward W. 124
Saint-Simon, Henri de 83
Salvini, Matteo 131
Schmidtke, Sabine 126
Schnädelbach, Herbert 60, 63
Scotland, Patricia 123
Şentürk, Recep 126
Sepúlveda, Juan G. de 44
Siep, Ludwig 61, 62
Smelser, Neil J. 51
Smith, Adam 32
Sommer, Maurie 15
Srinivasan, Thirukodikaval N. 27
Steinberg, Samuel H. 45
Stepan, Alfred 26
Strauss, Bruno 79
Strenski, Ivan 40
Susser, Bernard 82
al-Suyūtī, Jalāl al-Dīn 112, 113

Taylor, Charles 12, 22, 30, 39
Tirosh-Samuelson, Hava 47
Toledano, Ehud 113
Tönnies, Ferdinand 82
Torpey, John 120
Toynbee, Arnold 109
Traina, Cristina L.H. 69

VanAntwerpen, Jonathan 26, 27
Vikør, Knut S. 16

Wainscott, Ann M. 121
Walker, Peter 131
Walzer, Michael 88–93
Waterbury, John 133
Weber, Max 19, 39
White, Harrison C. 38
Winter, Tim (Abdal Hakim Murad) 14, 95
Wright, Robin 129
Wuhl, Simon 92

Žalec, Bojan 73
Zaret, David 30

Finito di stampare nel mese di giugno 2020
presso NotizieDue, Modena

www.ingramcontent.com/pod-product-compliance
Lightning Source LLC
Chambersburg PA
CBHW031835230426
43669CB00009B/1356